# Judaism and Anthroposophy

# Judaism and Anthroposophy

Edited by

Fred Paddock and Mado Spiegler

SteinerBooks

2003

*This publication was made possible with the generous support of*
ROBERT DULANEY

Our warmest thanks go to the following journals for permission
to translate and excerpt articles:

*Das Goetheanum*, Postfach, CH-4143 Dornach 1 www.goetheanum.ch/wocheschrift

*Info3*, Kirchgartenstr. 1 D 60439 Frankfurt/Main, www.info3.de

*Jarbuch für anthroposophische Kritik*, Lorenzo Ravagli editor, Trimethius Verlag/
Kunigundenstr. 4 80802 Munchen

*Novalis* (formerly *Die Kommenden*), Michael Frensch editor, Herblinger strasse 9,
CH 08238 Busingen Postfach 600, novalis@spectraweb.ch

*The Golden Blade*, Floris Books, Edinburgh, Scotland, www.florisbooks.co.uk


Published in cooperation with the Rudolf Steiner Library by
SteinerBooks, 400 Main Street, Great Barrington, MA 01230

www.steinerbooks.org

10 9 8 7 6 5 4 3 2 1

# Contents

# Preface

THE THOUGHT OF A PUBLICATION consisting of English translations of articles from top European anthroposophical journals has haunted me for thirty years. It has been quite clear that English-speaking anthroposophists are largely cut off from the truly extraordinary thought occurring on the continent.

All sorts of factors made this project untenable for many years. But now, many things have transpired to allow this dream to materialize. And not simply to materialize, but to help define the nature and direction of what at first was quite amorphous.

Four journals in particular showed me that there was an enormous amount of material that would be of real interest to Americans, and helped clarify and focalize the direction our prospective journal would take. One of these, *Novalis*, began ten years ago under the editorship of Michael Frensch as the successor to *Die Kommenden*. It refined, deepened, and both broadened and narrowed the editorial policy of the latter, which had mainly aimed at presenting current political and cultural events, personalities, and movements seen through the lens of anthroposophy. *Novalis* has downplayed the political in favor of the cultural, and broadened the sense of "current" to take in a range of historical backgrounds.

Another inspiring journal is *Info 3*. It, like *Novalis*, is carrying on a most informative and exciting conversation with the world around us.

The third journal is *Jahrbuch für Anthroposophische Kritik*, which was created to give anthroposophical scholars and researchers a chance to critique one another's work in order to raise the standard of anthroposophical writing to a level where it would be respected by scholars worldwide.

The fourth journal is *Das Goetheanum*. Some may consider this "official" journal of the society, by definition, a conservative and self-absorbed, dedicated to the internal concerns of organized anthroposophy—but during the 1990s it became an exciting, concerned-with-the-world publication.

Then translators appeared—in particular, my coeditor, Mado Spiegler. Others also offered their help, and they are identified with their bylines. In addition to translators, people with editorial and production skills turned up, and, last but not least, financial help was offered. With so much content and assistance converging to make this enterprise possible, one can see why I felt there was a clear calling to get this project going *now.*

Speaking of "calling" leads me to a most important element in making this collection possible—a shift within the Anthroposophical Society from an old task well done to a new task urgently beckoning. This shift has been most clearly stated by Reijo Wilenius, former head of the society in Finland, in an article that first appeared in *Anthroposophy Worldwide*, was reproduced in the newsletter of the American society, and then in the most recent issue of our Library Newsletter (no. 25/26). He credits the past leadership of the society—both national and international—with miraculously healing what has been a severely fragmented society: "It has rarely happened in the history of the world that a fragmented spiritual movement has been able to reunite. Yet in the case of the Anthroposophical Society, this wonder did occur." But this reintegration was not, for Wilenius, an end in itself. Rather, it was an essential stage that made possible the next step in anthroposophy's task—the step that we are *called upon* to take now. Listen to how Wilenius puts it: "Now, after experiencing this process of internal integration..., I have the impression that *the Being Anthroposophia wants to connect herself more with the world outside the Anthroposophical Society.* After the inner integration, it is time for the outer integration. It is time, as Rudolf Steiner put it [and as Arthur Zajonc, former leader of the American society, keeps reminding us] to 'grow together with the world.'" It is this "calling" of anthroposophy—working through the fine European journals, the generosity of translators, editors, designers, donors, and through the very ethos of the membership at large—that has made the appearance of this publication possible and given it its fundamental direction.

In response to this calling we have selected content with an eye for its pedagogical value to the large group of anthroposophists and friends who do not read German. We think you will appreciate, as we do, the depth, quality, and fairness of the authors' engagement with the diverse intellectual and spiritual movements within the different world cultures. Enjoy!

FRED PADDOCK

## Rabbi Nehorai Said:

Seek out a place of Torah,
where companions struggle together
in the pursuit of Truth.

Do not presume Torah will come to you;
you must go to her.

Ignorance is as natural as wisdom, and
the difference between them is not always clear.

Do not rely solely on your own understanding,
for there is no one easier to fool than yourself.

Do not rely solely on authority
nor be content with hallowed opinion,
for authority serves only authority.

Only attend to Reality
with fullness of mind, heart, and action
and experience what is for yourself.

IV:18

(From the *Pirke Avot*—the book of ethics in the
Mishnah—a modern reading by Rabbi Rami M. Shapiro,
published under the title *Wisdom of the Jewish Sages*)

# Introduction

RUDOLF STEINER'S REPEATED insistence that every phenomenon can fruitfully be approached from multiple points of view is all the more daunting in that it seems both self-evident and elusive to our twenty-first century minds: we approach the task with easy confidence, often failing to notice that we are merely craning our necks to get a better view. More often than not, we are standing on tiptoes, looking over the wall of familiar rationalizations. The daring ones among us may actually open the doors and windows, allow fresh air to circulate through the furnishings of our mind, without really moving out of the perimeter of our accustomed rounds.

If we take the challenge seriously, we soon discover how hard it is to thoroughly open up to another person's experience, without losing track of ourselves or of the multiple intersections revealed by the meeting of the perspectives. One area where this effort is both necessary and difficult has been anthroposophy's relationship with world religions. Even speaking of anthroposophy and *other* religions contradicts Steiner's own emphasis that—the "centrality" of the Mystery of Golgotha notwithstanding—anthroposophy was not a new religion, nor a superior one, nor should anthroposophists see themselves as the latest twist in the history of Christian denominations.

Instead, "in order to understand the spirit and core of anthroposophy ... anthroposophists must extend ... the strength and love working in the Gospels to the understanding of all religions."[1] Steiner also describes the relationship between, "a Buddhist who is an anthroposophist and a Christian who is an anthroposophist" as one in which each person "finds a way to the other's heart and believes (wills himself to believe) what the other believes, making an effort to "grasp the innermost core ... the essence, of each religion."[2]

Our relationship to history comes under the same injunction and is similarly handicapped: a conscious effort to understand the substance of historical epochs or individualities is often short-circuited by superficial enthusiasm for the picturesque differences between epochs, or distracted by more or less benign versions of the crude cultural evolutionism characteristic of modernity.

As Steiner pointed out, it would be true but misleading to say that humanity moves forward through a succession of "great spiritual leaders who are saying essentially the same thing though it takes different forms.... proclaiming different aspects of the same truth.... While quite true, this statement could scarcely be more trivial."[3]

Over the past decades, anthroposophists and others have paid increased attention to this demand that we fully

---

1. *The Gospel of St. Mark*, Rudolf Steiner, Lecture 3, Anthroposophic Press, 1986, p. 63.
2. Ibid., p. 61.
3. The extended comparison between Socrates and the Buddha in Lecture 4 of *The Gospel of St. Mark* (p. 68 ff.) and almost the entirety of Lecture 7 are good examples of Steiner's method.

experience both the oneness of religions and their individuality. The translations we present here are part of a growing body of German writings applying this approach to the question of Judaism and anthroposophy.

For historical reasons, Judaism has not been a very visible presence in anthroposophy, despite the fact that the Kabbalah has been a major contributor to Christian theosophy, and despite the fact that Central European Jews represented an important segment of the early anthroposophical movement.[4] To the extent that anthroposophy was anchored in German-speaking cultural areas, Jewish anthroposophists fell under the same spell as German-speaking Jews in general. While some managed to stay in Switzerland, many others went into exile in Britain or South America, New Zealand or Australia. Unspecified numbers of them disappeared in concentration camps. Those who survived and went to Israel were often unacknowledged due to their paradoxical position as "Christianized Jews with a love of German culture."

When interest in these issues awakened in recent years, it came with the heavy baggage of questions about the Holocaust, and of the responsibility of Central European culture (anthroposophists included) for anti-Semitism. Difficult as it may be to look at any historical moment with a really free eye, this is doubly true of the Holocaust. In this case, that Rudolf Steiner might have been associated with anti-Semitic statements, or even with ambiguous ones, was a possibility few anthroposophists were ready to consider. This is hardly surprising given the emotional load of the Holocaust for late twentieth-century souls, and in particular for men and

---

4. There were practicing Jews and kabbalists from Eastern Europe as well as highly assimilated Jews from Austria and Germany, some but not all of them baptized. Also, members of assimilated Western Jewish families who, like the Spanish *conversos* had retained some Jewish family rituals even when they had converted to Christianity. Rudi Lissau's is a vivid account of one such family.

women from the German cultural sphere. Yet the question refused to go away and the debate remains open.

Over the years, the reflection has been enriched by (and has in turn enriched) the general development of research in the mass of Steiner archives. New perspectives were provided by recent biographies. Most relevant in this respect was Lindenberg's biography[5] with its emphasis on Rudolf Steiner's life as a life in motion, his thinking as an evolving one. While Lindenberg himself did not directly answer (or even attempt to answer) the questions raised by the controversies, he paved the way for a thorough re-examination of Steiner as literary and political commentator, teacher, and spiritual master, thinking and acting in response to particular social environments.

This volume is devoted to various layers of this relationship. The volume is bracketed by two articles that represent a larger questioning about anthroposophy's relationship with world religions in general and Christianity in particular. Johannes Schneider looks at the resonance of Christian themes in contemporary world culture and the problematic promise of anthroposophy as a "Christology." Dierk Lorenz's iconoclastic piece denounces anthroposophists' reluctance to look at the possibility of anti-Semitism in their ranks, but does so out of a concern that this is really a reluctance to renounce the cozy temptations of institutionalized religion. The remaining chapters examine, in a variety of voices, some actual intersections of Judaism and esoteric Christianity.

We have, for example, Hugo Bergman's meditation on the act of blessing as Jewish "signature"; Shimon Levy's stories on the experience of Judaism as the history of the human "I," starting with the prophet Samuel as a youth; Rudi Lissau's evocative reflection on a life shaped and lived as a Christian and a Jew in a "first generation" anthroposophical family; and

---

5. Christoph Lindenberg, *Rudolf Steiner—Eine Biographie*, Freies Geistesleben, 1997.

Samuel Ichmann's pondering of his experience as a Waldorf school teacher encountering what might be called a kind of "folk anthro-christianity," the unthinking acceptance of well-meaning stereotypes and a naive belief that anthroposophy is identical with *some* form of organized Christianity.

Another series of articles explores some key concepts and paths of mutual influence in the conversation between Judaism and anthroposophy. Ruth Windolf examines aspects of the Greek and Hebrew language and thought. Other articles present aspects of kabbalistic tradition that will seem both very familiar and very remote. Christian kabbalists were attracted to Jewish mysticism by the latter's prefiguration of trinitarian thinking, in which they saw an early evolutionary stage of full-blown Christianity. Rolf Umbach's analysis of Sephirotic imagery leads us to the reading of a trinitarian configuration in the Sephirot tree, which in turn leads us to Christianity's *Logos*. When Princess Antonia of Wurttemberg commissioned the learning triptych described by Rolf Umbach, she intended it to be a graphic representation of the bridges between Old and New Testaments, expressing in images mysteries inexpressible in words. The Princess belonged to a generation of Christian theosophists who actively cultivated Jewish philosophy and imagery.

From there, we go on to follow the life-path of two individuals who saw themselves as bridges between Anthroposophy and Judaism: Ernst Müller, Viennese translator of the Sephirot into German, early Zionist, and one of Steiner's earliest and lifelong followers; and the Israeli philosopher Hugo Bergman, scholarly and political collaborator of Martin Buber and Gershom Scholem, translator of Steiner's work into modern Hebrew, and teacher of courses on Steiner's *Philosophy of Freedom*.

Rounding out this collection, we have Ralf Sonnenberg's account of the way Enlightenment philosophy paved the way for modern anti-Semitism, in a first take on what has become his lifework as a historian of nineteenth- and twentieth-century German culture, as well as Janos Darvas' biography of Francois-

Xavier Molitor—an intriguing portrait of a German idealist whose life was devoted to use and maintain the still existing bridges between the Kabbalah and Christianity, even while around him modern anti-Semitism was slowly taking root.

Rabbi Yannai said:

It is not within our grasp to explain the
prosperity of the wicked
or the suffering of the righteous.
All we are called upon to do
is to act justly ourselves.

Reality is more complex than we would like.
If we insist upon it making sense,
we will find ourselves despairing.
Reality cannot be neatly packaged,
bound with the ribbon of morality.
Reality is greater than our ideas of good and
evil;
Reality is beyond our right and wrong.
Reality is all that is, and this is often at odds
with what we imagine it should be.

Where we can stand up for justice, let us act.
Where we are confounded by Truth,
let us keep silent.

IV:19

(From the *Pirke Avot*)

# I

# CHRISTIANITY AND OTHER RELIGIONS:
## DOES ANTHROPOSOPHIC CHRISTOLOGY CREATE A BARRIER FOR NON-CHRISTIAN CULTURES?

## BY JOHANNES W. SCHNEIDER

*from* Das Goetheanum, *June 11, 2000*

*abstract by Henry Jaeckel*

ALTHOUGH THE IDENTIFICATION of Christianity with colonialism had seemed to condemn it to lasting rejection, it is also the case that wherever Christianity is lived in a convincing manner, it is acknowledged and respected. Thus at the time of Mother Teresa's death, an Arabic newspaper reported, "She was a devout Catholic, but her impressive way of life led her beyond the immediate connection with her particular religion. Her message and her actions reached every human being on Earth." In another example, the Burmese General Tim Oo, later a leader of the Movement for Democracy, reported reading the Gospels in jail: "I read the sayings of Christ, and I found this man's teaching very Buddhist!"

Even more important than those statements about individuals or about the contents of Christianity, we find in Islamic countries the tendency represented by the Iranian philosopher Abdolkarim Sorush. He opposes to fundamentalism the need for a rediscovery by Islam of an individual religiosity of the type represented by the Sufis in the past. In 1997, the newly elected president of Iran, Khatami, pleaded for a searching, questioning Islam, as opposed to sclerotic fundamentalism. Whenever a person is in motion, he or she finds the dialogue with others possible, beyond the boundaries of worldviews.

It is also of note that in China there is a search for spirituality, especially among the intelligentsia. Against a perceived failure by Communism to provide credible meaning to human existence, Chinese people are looking elsewhere, primarily toward Christianity.

Do these developments allow us to claim that other religions are opening toward Christianity? The answer is no, but contacts and meaningful discussion have become more frequent. It is also important to hear similar sounds coming from the Catholic Church. John Paul II stated recently in Manila that it is possible to be a genuine Christian and a genuine Chinese at the same time, because Christ's message belongs to all.

What, actually, is anthroposophic Christology? We might start by pointing out that the mere existence of the Christian church is not the stumbling block for other cultural circles: the point of contention is the Christian statement: "Christ is risen! Christ is a God-being, Christ is with us!" These are all statements that are strongly emphasized by anthroposophy.

Why, we may ask, should this view of Christ create problems? The answer is that when Christians speak about the God-nature of the presently active risen Christ, others get the impression that Christians claim to possess a final truth that other religions do not possess. Some streams of Buddhism see Gautama Buddha as a kind of divine being. Inside each human being there is a hidden Buddha-nature that can be awakened through meditation. The reason this statement seems less controversial is because it is connected with lived experience rather than dogma.

In the same way, anthroposophic Christianity stresses the need for an individual Christ-experience, and for the recognition of the activity of the resurrected Christ on Earth today.

Each Christ-experience on this path will be individually colored, and no one can claim general validity for what they have seen. Nonetheless, these experiences can be recognized by all who have had similar encounters. From the point of view of anthroposophic Christology, it is a matter of observing and understanding the working of Christ in each individual, including ourselves. Christ appears individually to many, whether they be Christian or non-Christian.

Anthroposophy is also especially concerned with the self-observation of the cognizing human being. It is in this sense that Rudolf Steiner emphasizes (in *The Philosophy of Freedom*[1]) the observation of one's own thinking as the door to spiritual experience.

It is not the purpose of anthroposophic Christology to proclaim eternal truths. Its purpose is, rather, to describe the path and the experiences of each individual human being in their quest for spiritual truth.

We may have something to learn about Christ from the surprised reaction of the Arabic commentator who felt Mother Teresa's message was meant for him personally. And if Tim Oo feels that the words of the Gospels are Buddhist, we can, perhaps, discover there a new nuance of Christianity.

The path of anthroposophic Christology begins with noticing and recognizing today's active Christ in ourselves. That is where we can experience Christ most directly. This path leads inevitably to exchanges of thoughts and experiences with others. Whoever can see the human being in others is on the way to recognizing the Christ.

An old Christian legend tells of a poor man who takes a beggar into his hut and shares his bed and meager meal with him.

---

1. Available as *Intuitive Thinking As a Spiritual Path*, Anthroposophic Press, 1995.

In the morning, when the poor man follows the departing beggar, he suddenly disappears from view. The poor man understands that his guest had been Christ.

Theologians have often criticized anthroposophic literature for not being precise enough regarding God and Christ. There is indeed a tendency in anthroposophic literature to speak about the "Christ impulse" if Christ himself is meant, and about an eternal "God-being" when God himself is meant. While the criticism may not be unjustified, it also reflects a misunderstanding of anthroposophy.

Theology's concern is the transmittal of God's revelations in a form that is generally valid. Anthroposophic Christology, on the other hand, aims primarily at providing a personal, that is, individual understanding of God's revelations through spiritual experiences. Such individual experiences are unique and cannot be repeated. This should show the misunderstanding contained in the dogmatic statement: "But Rudolf Steiner said...," which one occasionally hears.

Rudolf Steiner followed one of the possible ways to the experience of Christ, an individual way, as individual as every path to the Christ-understanding must be. Anthroposophic theology is not a substitute for theology, though it can be a complement to it. Furthermore, anthroposophic Christology is not a path for everybody, but a path for those who want to start out from their own observations, including the realm of religion. It is the path of modern human beings, those who have the strength for individualization—that is, those who are free from dogma, people like Abdolkarim Sorush.... When followed honestly and consistently, the anthroposophic path of cognition reveals how the human being is embedded in divine activity, with the result that cognition becomes a religious act. Aristotle said that the cognition of the divine is a human being's real prayer. Rudolf Steiner carries this thought further when he says: Whenever meditative cognition has developed into the state of inspiration, thinking becomes praying.

It is the specific task of anthroposophic Christology to transform the already cognizing human being. Anthroposophy as a way of cognition leads to a religious stance that carries forward the human being who had evolved through an orientation toward the earth. This task could not be carried out if anthroposophy was turned into a dogma.

Another way to develop one's religious insight is by contemplating the inherent depth of the images of the revelations, as was beautifully demonstrated by the Swedish writer Selma Lagerlöf in her *Christ Legends*.[2] From her, anthroposophists can learn spiritual modesty—and also, how unpretentious perceptions can be illuminated by experiences on the christological path of cognition.

We human beings need one another.

Rabbi Tarfon said:

The day is short.
The task is great.
The workers are lazy.

The stakes are high.
The employer — impatient!

Time is fleeting.
Now is eternal.
Discipline yourself to attention,
for the alternative is despair.

II:19

(From the *Pirke Avot*)

---

2. *The Emperor's Vision and Other Christ Legends*, Floris Books, 2002.

# 2

# On Judaism

BY Günther Röschert

*from* Jahrbuch für Anthroposophische Kritik, 1994
*translated by Magdalene Jaeckel and Fred Paddock*

*If you think yourself better than the others,*
*don't forget that it is not you who sustains the root,*
*but it is the root that sustains you.*

—Romans 11,18

## 1. Ezra[1]

In the middle of the sixth century BC, after his decisive victory over the Babylonians, King Cyrus of Persia declared an end to the Jewish exile and granted the Jews the right to rebuild their temple in Jerusalem.

Some Jews moved back, but there was no massive movement of return. Conditions had changed in Palestine during the long Jewish exile. Many Jews had remained there, and settled down in the countryside or in the neighborhood of the destroyed city of Jerusalem, but religious rituals were no longer performed. Many migrants from neighboring lands had moved into the Southern Kingdom of Judah, making the area into a heterogeneous country.

---

1. Precise information about Ezra's identity, dates and mandate is problematic, due to contradictions between the books of Ezra and Nehemia and the Chronicles. The Apocryphal Book IV, Book of Ezra is totally unusable for historical questions.

The rebuilding of the temple started with great enthusiasm, only to falter after a while. Judah remained a protectorate of the Persian rulers of Syria. It seemed questionable whether there could again be a Jewish community founded on the old covenant of God and Moses on Mount Sinai. How could such a mixed population uphold the idea of being God's chosen people? Into this situation, the priest and scholar Ezra entered the picture: under the tolerant regime of King Artaxerxes, he undertook to consolidate conditions in Palestine so as to prevent a recurrence of what had happened to the ten northern tribes, which had dissolved into the melting pot of western Asia after the Assyrian deportation.

Ezra was able to build on the foundation of a synagogue transformed by exile into a lay institution of learning and prayer. The synagogue thus became a decentralized religious institution independent of the temple. Ezra reunited the Jewish people in a solemn dedication to the law of the Torah. He forbade all new mixed marriages and annulled all existing ones.[2]

Ezra and Nehemiah's reforms were followed by a long period in which the main role was played by an association of teachers of the Torah, the "Wise Men of Israel," also called *Perushim*— Greek for "the Pure"—(hence the name Pharisees). This organization of the Pharisees, from which the rabbinate eventually arose, guaranteed the preservation of Ezra's inheritance and enabled the people of the Torah to survive till this day.

## HALACHAH

The core of the Jewish religion is the Torah; the core of the Christian religion is Jesus Christ. The Hebrew Bible is for the Jew the central and final revelation of God. There need be no additional revelation, only continued exegesis and interpretation. The first compilation of existing materials took place in

---

2. To what extent the rules were actually applied over the centuries is debatable.

the seventh century BCE with Deuteronomy, to be supplemented later by the four books of Moses (Genesis, Exodus, Leviticus, and Numbers). Together these five books constitute the Five Books of Moses, or the Torah. In Ezra's time, the biblical canon became a normative collection of historical, poetic, and prophetic writings, wisdom literature, and the actual teachings of the Pentateuch. More materials were added through the first century BCE, while a wide field of apocalyptic texts were kept out of the canon by consensus. The central theme of the Hebrew Bible is God's taking the Israelites out of Egypt. This led to Moses receiving the Torah from the hand of God on Mount Sinai. The original Torah consisted of the Ten Commandments, to which were added various rules of conduct given to Moses for his people.

The law of the Torah was the foundation of religious and political life in the old nation of Israel. From the beginning, the Jews emphasized the daily conduct of life, not doctrinal contents. The laws of the Pentateuch had to be applied not only to the individual's everyday life, but also to all significant proceedings of the state. From the Jewish standpoint, it was inconceivable that any of life's problems might be resolved without recourse to the Torah, for God's law has no gaps. Therefore, the wise men who could interpret the law and apply it to any given life situation were highly regarded. It is the undeniable achievement of Pharisaic society to have started the tradition of the "unwritten Torah," which is continued to this day by the rabbis in every Jewish community devoted to the Torah. Until the end of the "rabbinical era" proper in the ninth century CE, the Palestinian and Babylonian Talmuds and many other exegeses developed in Palestine and Babylon: they represent a tremendous treasure of life wisdom and ethical experience, accumulated for the benefit of all of humankind. The term *halachah* refers to the practical part of the written and unwritten Torah. *Halachah* is the expression of pharisaic spirituality, but its teachings are not just the accumulation of legal decisions. *Halachah itself is Torah.* It is said to have lain hidden in the revelation of Sinai, to be gradually discovered by the rabbis' thinking and discussion. This process of interpretation of the revelation is an ongoing process, and it will continue as long as there is Judaism oriented to the Torah. God's word, the Torah, is eternal, and no amount of comments, explanations, or interpretations can ever reach more than a small part of its true depth, even though thousands of years of studies by the sages of Israel have constantly increased its riches.

We are not, thus, dealing with mere intellectual games of refining through analogy and paradox, but rather with Israel's conviction that every step in life is an opportunity as well as a commitment to discern and carry out God's will. The Judaism that—after 1800 years of exile—turned back to the building of a Jewish state was therefore at its core halachah-Judaism, the form of life of those whose deeds are rooted in the knowledge of the Torah.[3]

## THE NEW TESTAMENT

When the Gospels mention Judaism, comments range from neutral to hostile; generally speaking, whatever is said about the teachers of the Torah (Scribes and Pharisees) is sharply critical. A concentration of negative pronouncements about Judaism can be found in the Gospels according to Matthew and John, but also in some of the letters of the apostle Paul.

Thus, in the parable of the murderous winegrowers (Matt. 23: 33-41), Jesus Christ describes Israel as a fruitful vineyard whose workers refuse to obey their master. They kill the

---

3. One of the ambiguities of Israel's foundation was that its original promoters and a sizable if shrinking proportion of its Jewish population rejected *halachah* and religious rituals as archaic remnants. Their goal was the building of a modern Jewish secular state on the same foundation and with the same justification as other newly founded nation-states. For historical reasons, of course, their own lives were in many cases rooted in *halachah*, and, most importantly, in the conception of the relation between sacred book, law, and interpretation as a sacred, ever-renewed duty. (translator's note—MS)

owner's messengers and even his son in order to inherit the vineyard, thus triggering gruesome retribution and the transmission of the inheritance to other, worthier, heirs. Elsewhere, Jesus calls the Pharisees hypocrites, closing to others the Kingdom of God while not deserving to enter it themselves. He calls down upon them and the leaders of the Jewish nation the blood of all the murdered righteous men since Abel.

Matthew (Matt. 27) refers to the horrible scene in front of Pilate's palace, when the Jews call down upon themselves the blood of Jesus. For centuries to come, Christian authors blithely interpreted this as the unqualified Jewish denial of the appearance of the Messiah whom the Jews themselves had so eagerly anticipated. For centuries to come, this passage served to justify their condemnation of the Jews as God's murderers.

With the introduction of "biblical criticism" by the Jewish philosopher Baruch Spinoza, different interpretive views became possible. People began to consider the possibility that anti-Judaic passages in the Gospels actually reflected a power struggle between a newly arising Christian church and its parent, the synagogue. This view, of course, required abandoning the dogma of a Holy Scripture whose every word was inspired. By now, this dogma has in fact been abandoned by Catholic and Protestant theologians alike, inasmuch as they have accepted that there is not only a divine, but also a human side of the Gospel. The text is now considered to be "historical" as well as '"revealed."

By itself, however, this can't answer the question as to the truth of the Gospel between divine revelation and human interpretation. While it has generally become accepted that the anti-Judaic tone of the Gospels applies to "Jews" as symbolic of humanity in general, real-life "Jews" are still seen as the part of humankind that, as Christ's sworn enemies, are headed toward eternal damnation.

In any case, reconsidering the anti-Judaism of the New Testament forces us to ask about the proper way to understand all revelation; a question which of course applies to the Torah as well, and which Spinoza himself had raised in precisely that way. Paul, a Pharisee himself despite his fanatical "anti-Pharisee" stance, saw his Jewish contemporaries' unwillingness to accept the message of Christ in the context of the heathens' greater openness to it. He had a vision of the Jews accepting their Messiah only after the majority of the heathens had already learned of him. This may explain his restless eagerness to spread the Gospel of the Risen Christ far and wide as fast as possible. Again and again, he bursts out in anger against his own people: "They have killed even Jesus, our Lord, and they persecute us. Their conduct does not please God and makes them the enemies of the whole human race" (1 Thess. 2: 15 ff.).

However inconsistent, the anti-Judaism in the New Testament had devastating consequences for the Jews' history in the West. Again and again, religious or pseudo-religious reasons were used to justify the oppression and segregation of the Jews, all the way to the horror of the pogroms and to the murder of millions. Even the demonic German dictator's hatred of the Jews played on such pseudo-religious connotations.[4]

The efforts of twentieth-century thinkers to point out the Jewishness of Jesus Christ, to bring him back, as it were, into the fold of his people, may be seen as signs that the ecumenical impulse of the Christ has now overcome the narrow-mindedness of the traditional Christian churches.

## JESUS WAS A JEW

The genealogies in Matthew and Luke's gospels show what great emphasis was put by the early church on the physical ancestry of Jesus. Only because of his purely Jewish blood could he be the Messiah. Among the disciples and apostles, there was no question as to the Jewishness of Jesus. In the Gos-

---

4. The fact that Hitler was personally hostile to Christianity, partly because it was a "judaized" religion, did not prevent him from using the old baggage of Christian anti-Semitism.

pel of John, Christ tells the Samaritan woman: "Salvation is from the Jews" (John 4, 22). It is absurd to skip Jesus' Jewish ancestry in order to make him into an abstractly generalized "universal human" figure. The universally human becomes concrete within a national community, or at least on its margins. Even the most convinced citizen of the world is, at core, a member of a nation. Only in the twentieth century does the national feeling itself become doubtful. The spiritual authority of the "Christ" (Greek: the "anointed one") comes from his being the Messiah, announced to and hoped for by the Jews. This is also what was meant by Peter's words in Matthew 16:16, "You are the Christ, the son of the living God!"

This also allows us to understand the words attributed to Christ, although their authenticity has been questioned: "Heaven and Earth may pass away before even the smallest letter of the law will pass away." "The law" here means the Torah. Why should the revelation of Sinai, the written and unwritten Torah, all of a sudden be abandoned because of the appearance of Christ? Had the rules of conduct of the Torah been wrong all along? Up to this day, pious Jews see no reason for abruptly giving up the Torah, God's word to his people. What should they exchange it for? Surely not for the belief in Jesus of Nazareth as the Messiah, in a world without peace and without righteousness that has brought their own people to the brink of destruction?

Paul was clearly wrong when he claimed that the Torah was by definition inapplicable, and could at best serve to reveal the sinful nature of all humankind. Jewish theologians' repeated efforts to explain the New Testament out of the Jewish tradition are of especially great value. Many Christians would be dismayed to discover how many misconceptions they harbor as a result of their ignorance of the Jewish background of their own faith. [5]

---

5. E.g., Pinkas Lapide, *Ist die Bibel richtig übersetzt?* (Is the Bible Translated Correctly?), Gütersloh, 1986.

No one wanting to meet Christ Jesus can bypass an encounter with Judaism, for Jewish heredity is the foundation for the resurrection-body on which the hopes of Christianity are built. Rudolf Steiner's "Fifth Gospel" lectures describe every phase of Jesus' life in such a way that his Jewishness is never doubted. The message is that Christ could not have incarnated into any nation other than the Jewish.

## THE WILL OF GOD

Like Islam, Judaism always stood firm for the uniqueness and singularity of God. It is really not accurate to say that the God of Israel was originally a "tribal God" that only later, through the teachings of the prophets, developed into the all-embracing creator of the world. In reality, the descriptions of creation in the oldest parts of the Bible contradict such an interpretation. Even though the earliest texts mention the special role of the Chosen People, this in no way reduces God to a kind of folk-spirit.

God's exalted position doesn't prevent him from giving his people very concrete, practical rules for the conduct of their daily lives. If prescriptions rooted in the revelation are to guide the conduct of human life, there needs to be an ongoing process of legal interpretation and creativity to adapt the law to the changing circumstances of human life. The Talmud is the product of this unending process.

On the surface, the Babylonian Talmud is a collection of anecdotes about Biblical questions, the fruit of Jewish rabbis' and teachers' labors over a thousand years. The Torah contains 613 rules: 365 prohibitions and 248 recommendations. Over the centuries, great prophets and rabbis reduced these to the most essential: David transmitted eleven laws in Psalm 15. Isaiah reduced them to two (Isaiah 56:1). Amos declares: "Thus speaks the Lord to the house of Israel: Seek me, and you will live" (Amos 5:4). Habakkuk, elaborating on Amos

says: "The unrighteous one will die; but the righteous will
live because of his faith" (Habakkuk 2,4). Paul's teaching
about salvation (Romans 1:17) is based on this passage by
Habakkuk.

Such a reduction of the Torah to a few basic divine laws is
not a mere concern of logic or dialectical analysis. The reduction leads into the mystical heart of the Torah.

Jesus Christ himself was questioned about the highest law.
"Rabbi, what do you hold to be the most important law of the
Torah?" He answered: "You shall love the Lord your God with
all your heart, with all your soul and with all your mind. This
is the first and greatest commandment, and a second is like
unto it. You shall love your neighbor as yourself. On these two
commandments hang all the Torah and the prophets" (Matt.
22:36). The Christ refers here to Israel's credo and central
prayer, the Sh'ma (Deuteronomy 6:4ff) and connects it to the
command to love our neighbor.

The Torah committed the Jewish people to the sacredness of
life. "Be holy, for I, your God, am holy" Lev. 19:2). This is the
source of joy in the commandments, the Torah joy, for the
Torah makes possible a life lived according to the Will of God.
The rabbis are convinced that a deed done out of obedience to
the Torah is of higher moral value than the same deed done out
of individual choice.

This seems to distance in the extreme Jewish ortho-praxis
(correct or healing action) from modern ethical autonomy and
individualism, for the latter is built not on revelation but on
the intuitive capacity of the moral self ("Ich" ["I"]). And yet
even Christ Jesus prayed: "Not mine but your will be done."
(Matt. 26:39). In the end, ethical individualism is legitimized
only to the extent that it discerns the traces of God's will latent
in the processes of the world and comes to meet this will half-
way with its own individual moral decisions. The things of the
world are the stuff of human deeds, but God sees into the
heart. The role of the heart in actions determined by ideals is

what Rudolf Steiner called "love for the deed." Here, he is close to the words of Christ in Matthew 22 as well as to Jewish Torah joy.

The foundation of rabbinical morality is not love, but righteousness. But this righteousness is the expression of the love of God.

## AHASVERUS

According to a legend coming down from the late Middle Ages, a man called Ahasverus refused the cross-carrying Jesus a short rest on the steps of his house. Having met Jesus' eyes, the man went on to wander the earth carrying around in himself an unending life, vainly seeking rest and forgiveness. He is the "Wandering Jew." Many cultures, of course, have such an archetypal figure of the eternally restless wanderer. But Christian propaganda used the archetypal story of Ahasverus for its own ends, seeing in Ahasverus the Jewish nation as a whole, forever restless without a homeland, owing to the curse that God had laid upon them. In recent times, it was the Nazis who made the "eternal Jew" into a slogan aimed at stirring up hatred and abetting their murderous intents. As a result, it is no longer possible to think of the relation between the legend of the ghostly Ahasverus and Judaism independently of the horror of the concentration camps, of the destruction of European Judaism.

The theme of Ahasverus figures in Rudolf Steiner's thinking over the years, starting in the 1890s, when he was publishing the *Magazine for Literature*. It took different connotations as Steiner's thinking evolved. Originally, independently of its religious components, Ahasverus represented, among other things, a positive quality of detachment from atavistic blood-based social organization. If Ahasverus had taken on a godlike quality, it was similar to the "godlike" quality of Nietzsche's Zarathustra. This "pulling oneself up by one's root" remained essential for humankind to evolve into the future.

Rudolf Steiner concerned himself with the figure of Ahasverus in lectures held in Bern (March 23, 1922)[6] and in Dornach (March 24, 1922). He characterized Ahasverus as a supersensible being: the anti-type of incarnated God, the human being as incomplete God. Ahasverus is "the guardian of Judaism" following the mystery of Golgotha. He has in an unlawful way become God; he has put aside the mortal nature of humankind. The Ahasverus figure wanders "from folk to folk." He does not "for example, allow the Hebrew faith to die."

Anyone taking a sympathetic interest in Ahasverus and his suffering will note that Judaism has a regular companion and helper, guardian and protector: the Prophet Elijah, the representative of the Jewish folk-soul.

Elijah belongs to those few figures in the Bible who were bodily taken up into the heavenly world. The relationship between Elijah and Ahasverus is striking because the great prophet also appears again and again on earth. Over thousands of years the Jewish people experienced the nearness of Elijah. The door of the Jewish house is open for him, his chair is ready, and the goblet awaits his hand. Elijah is also (for Muslims) Al-Khadir (Chidher, the Green Prophet), the guardian of the waters of immortal life. The mysterious triad *Ahasverus-Elijah-Chidher* may be seen as a reference to the resurrection body, perceived as God's image in supersensible bodily form, rather than as the preservation of mineral contents.

---

6. *Man's Soul-Life in Sleeping, Waking, Dreaming*, March 21, 1922; and *The Mystery of Golgotha and Its Relation to Human Sleep*, March 24, 1922. (Editor's Note: other sources are based on incomplete or corrupted stenographer's notes.) A book published in 1930 by the Jewish anthroposophist Ludwig Thieben was considered difficult at the time of its publication and is now considered scandalous in its ignorance of Judaism. Its reprinting in 1991 was among the incidents that raised questions about anthroposophic anti-Semitism. Röschert's original footnote to this article call it "interesting material on 'anthroposophical opinion-making.'"

As Steiner formulated it, Ahasverus is the imagination of an aspect of the Jewish folk-destiny. In so far as he does not let the Hebrew faith die, he is the bearer of a positive mission. The spiritual foundation of the history of the Jewish exile is the Torah. Ahasverus must thus be thought of in connection with the Torah. Even the Shekinah, the presence of God, lives in exile. The Shekinah's reflection lives on the written surface of the Torah scrolls, which are preserved in every synagogue throughout the world.

## ISRAEL

Thirty-seven years after the Passover during which Christ was crucified, the great catastrophe descended upon the Holy City, interpreted by the Christians as the fulfillment of Christ's prophetic words of woe over Jerusalem mentioned in Matthew 21:20-24 (which was, of course, written *after* the fall of Jerusalem). The Roman general Titus Flavius suppressed the Jewish revolt by destroying the city as well as Herod's temple and driving out the entire Jewish population. The year 70 AD marks the beginning of the Jewish diaspora, the scattering of the Jewish people all over the world.

More than 1800 years later, on May 14, 1948, David Ben-Gurion proclaimed the Jewish state of Israel in Tel Aviv. Martin Buber, the greatest thinker of the young state, always maintained that the only place where this state could exist was in Palestine, while at the same time warning that the Jewish people should never neglect their spiritual mission, lest they should ultimately perish. Today's Israel is a democracy with an extremely heterogeneous population. Orthodox and free thinkers confront each other. Yet, in Israel, the anticipation of the Messiah is not dead. The people still await the priestly hero who is to change all life on earth.

The anticipation of the Messiah is the most precious legacy of the Jewish people for all humankind: the present conditions on earth are by definition temporary, and no human rule is ever legitimate unless it obeys the ideal of justice. Any sacralization of human power necessarily collides with God. When Christians think that the Messiah has already come but the Jews didn't recognize him, this is only half the truth, for Christians themselves are still awaiting the Second Coming "in the clouds of heaven." As eschatological hope waned, the churches narrowed Christian thinking by only considering Christ's life on earth, his passion, crucifixion, and resurrection. The mood of quiet anticipation could unite Christians and Jews.

Starting in 1910, Rudolf Steiner described the approach of the Christ toward the earthly sphere (GA118). The time he referred to is also the time during which Israel found an earthly home again. The reappearance of Israel in Palestine is considered an eschatological sign of the nearness of the Messiah. It may well be that Israel's mission is not limited to the establishment of its own state in that region, although non-Jews should not take this as a justification for denying Israel's right to existence. The painful confrontation between Arabs and Jews, for which Europeans should bear some responsibility, is in some ways the negative of Israel's potential mediation between East and West, North and South.

Shimon ben Gamliel said:

I grew up among the Sages.
All my life I listened to their words.
Yet I have found nothing better than silence.

Study is not the goal, doing is.
Do not mistake "talk" for "action."
Pity fills no stomach.
Compassion builds no house.
Understanding is not justice.

Whoever multiplies words causes confusion.
The truth that can be spoken
is not the Ultimate Truth.
Ultimate Truth is wordless,
the silence within the silence.

More than the absence of speech,
More than the absence of words,
Ultimate Truth is the seamless being-in-place
that comes with attending to Reality.

1:17

(From the *Pirke Avot*)

# 3

# The Hebrew Experience of Reality
## as contrasted with the Greek[1]

## by Ruth Windolf

*from Novalis, July-August, 1998*

*translated by Peter Luborsky*

Two familiar but contrasting images: the standing Socrates, sunk deep in thought; the davening Jew, swaying back and forth in prayer. In them, two different approaches to reality are manifested: the Greek, at rest and stationary; the Hebrew, dynamic and mobile. Years ago a Norwegian theologian named Thorleif Boman wrote a scholarly book undertaking a highly differentiated study, with numerous examples, demonstrating the great difference between Greek and Hebrew thought. In the New Testament these two meet side by side, mixing sometimes harmoniously, sometimes in a harmony of contrasts, but always in Hellenized form.

Like no other, these two approaches to the world have set their stamp on Western culture, though they are unevenly represented. Unfortunately Boman's trailblazing work was scarcely noticed outside of scholarly circles; and incomprehensibly, even there it led to no further questioning or research in

---

1. This article is essentially a reading of Thorleif Boman's *Hebrew Thought Compared with Greek*, 1960, still considered the classic philological study of the differences between Hebrew and Greek thought. Unless otherwise indicated, all quotes are assumed to be from this book.

the area, let alone to a correction of our one-sidedly Greek image of God and the human being. As I attempted to grasp the chief lines of thought in his book, my area of inquiry expanded along with my personal experiences and thoughts (through a number of extended visits in Israel, conversations with Jews, reading Jewish literature—particularly Abraham Joshua Heschel—and studying modern Hebrew). I found that even the vocabulary we use so unquestioningly is actually of Greek origin: "image of God," "image of man," "edifice of faith"—but more on this later.

## Thought: Static / Dynamic

The Greek's thinking is oriented toward harmony, eternal Ideas, beauty, measure, order, logic and resting-in-Being, and this finds vivid expression in the harmony of their temples and sculptures. The Hebrew approach to reality, in contrast, emphasizes the dynamic. Even the verb forms of the language reveal it, their basic meaning always expressing a motion or power. Movement and stasis, for example, are experienced not as opposites but as complementary. In the building of a house until it stands finished, movement and stasis are united. Even today in *Ivrit* (modern Hebrew), the word for marriage is "peace." To Hebrew understanding, this implies reaching peace, no matter out of how much movement.

To the Greek mind, the only thing that exists is Being without movement or change; all becoming and passing away is mere illusion, a nothingness about which nothing positive can be said. The impressions of our senses are deceptive. We see how un-Greek and incomprehensible to the Greeks themselves it was that the Hebrews accorded such great respect and importance to the dynamic, to movement.

Heraclitus, with his doctrine "everything flows; no one can step in the same river twice," is quite an isolated figure. Plato recognized him as such, but was unable to categorize him.

Greek thinking is oriented toward the true-ness of a thought. The Hebrew approach is oriented toward doing. It moves from the general to the particular, seeking the most direct path to realization of the deed. The dynamic element of movement and the static element of rest are the red threads running through the two different approaches to reality.

Hebrew thinking is directed toward making-concrete. It is rich in adjectives, not systematic, not discursive, not logical, but intuitive, personalistic, analytical, psychological in its approach to understanding, and more person-oriented than thing-oriented—in other words, not functional. "To the Hebrew mind, a thing that displays no qualities is a nothing." In the Psalms and in the Song of Solomon we constantly encounter a kind of adjectival language that obviously does not intend to give a description, but to render a reality.

## LOGOS — DABHAR

Throughout the East, a dynamic power was ascribed to the word—in particular the word out of God's mouth. The Egyptians and Mesopotamians, who put down so much in writing, have left plentiful evidence of this belief; and doubtless the Hebrews were confirmed and strengthened there in their characteristic belief in the central significance of the word. Boman gives an example from the great Sumerian hymn to Enlil: His word breaks great trees, His word is an approaching flood, against which no resistance will avail. The Old Testament tells us: "Is not my word like fire," says the Lord, "and like a hammer that breaks a rock in pieces?" (Jeremiah 23, 29) and in Isaiah 9,8: "The Lord sent a word into Jacob, and it hath lighted upon Israel."

The Hebrew for "word" is *dabhar*. *Dabhar* means not only "word," however; it also signifies word as deed, as occurrence, and as thing. For the Hebrew, "the word is the highest and noblest function of the human being and is therefore identical with his deed." Thus word and deed are not two different meanings of *dabhar*; rather, "deed" flows out of the basic meaning that resides in *dabhar*.

In this sense an ineffective word is an empty word. As the word implies and contains the doing, Goethe's rendering of John I,I in Faust, *Im Anfang war die Tat* ("In the beginning was the deed"), reveals one facet of the original meaning in a profoundly accurate way. Through the Septuagint our concept of the original word has been reduced to that of Greek *logos*, which contains gathering, ordering, calculating, speaking, and thinking, but has nothing to do with deed-power.

The following schema by Thorlief Boman lays out the two distinct approaches that meet in the word, though they move in different directions.

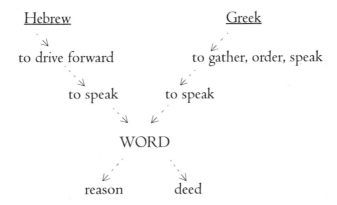

What is important to the Greeks is that the word *is:* It has Beingness ("The logos expresses the existent as it is."— Plato, Crat. 385b).

The difference between the two thought-worlds lies in their effect. "The dynamic of the Hebrew noun is active, visible, and sensible, like the deeds of the Oriental." The dynamic of the Greek Ideas is like "the action of magnets and the sun—passive and invisible, but still very real. The magnet attracts iron while resting immobile. The sun raises water into the air through evaporation, and the rain from the clouds gives all life

the power to grow. Yet the sun remains motionless and quiet."
In a certain respect, *logos* is a passive concept, in any case, an
intellectual one. Doing is not an essential attribute of it, as it is
of the *dabhar*. Pinchas Lapide never tired of emphasizing that
the verb Jesus used by far most frequently was "do."

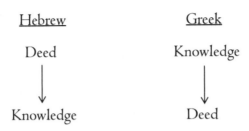

| Hebrew | Greek |
|--------|-------|
| Deed | Knowledge |
| ↓ | ↓ |
| Knowledge | Deed |

Moses said to the people gathered in the desert: "All that the
Lord has spoken, ye shall do and hear" (Exodus 24,7). The
standard translation has "ye shall do, ye shall be obedient,"
which shows that the translators did not understand what was
really meant. The fact of the matter is that to appreciate, hear,
understand, or perceive is often the consequence of a foregoing
activity. It is only when I have had some experience skiing, driving, or surfing the web that I begin to develop a real interest in
doing it; through deed-directedness my awareness and sensibil-
ity begin to grow in a way they never could out of a purely
abstract interest.

## IMPRESSION AND APPEARANCE

The Hebrews were not interested in an exact photographic
impression of an object or a person. How a thing is made
interested them, and the dynamic power of a person. When
Noah's ark is to be built, exact indications are given: The frame
is to be built using a certain type of wood and sealing material,
and so on (Gen. 6,14). The same was true of the Ark of the
Covenant (Ex. 25-28): the way it should be made is described
in painstaking detail, but we never are told how the completed

ark looked in the end. Very much the same applies to individuals who are called "beautiful," such as Potiphar's wife, Saul and David.... The Hebrew avoids giving a detailed description, preferring comparisons, symbols, or analogies. Like the Greeks, the Hebrews recognized beauty as "the spiritual manifesting within the sensible." To the Hebrew, however, beauty is not form, as it is to the Greeks; it stimulates. So little value was placed on form among the Hebrews that no words developed among them for shape, outline, or contour. Things and people do not possess such a delimited selfhood or individuality. Togetherness and interdependence occupy a more prominent place in their consciousness. Limitlessness and infinity pose no problem to the Hebrews!

The Greeks were fascinated by form—and not only the timeless form of geometric structures. The purpose of the flutings in the Ionic column, for example, was to lend more plasticity to its beauty by capturing light and shadow. This need for beauty and harmony called forth among them many architects and sculptors of the highest caliber. To them, as the Platonic philosophy puts it, "beauty was nothing relative, but an absolute quantity. When I behold beauty (the True, the Good, and the Beautiful) and receive it into myself, I draw near to the divinity." This triad forms an inseparably unity. The Hebrews want to be seized by beauty through all their senses. Sensations are the mediators—sensations that come from stimuli, from the power, charm, smell, or taste of something. The object need not be beautiful in its form: it might be the awe-inspiring fire or the hurricane that devastates trees.

Here again the crucial aspect is that we are moved inwardly by beauty and power, not that we rest in harmony and beauty.

Quite early on, before Yahweh united aspects of the many gods in himself, becoming the strongest and the sole one to whom homage was due, the Hebrews renounced creating any sort of image of their God ("Thou shalt not make any graven image"). They chose symbols: a candelabra, the Holy Ark of the Torah, the Torah scroll, a hand indicating God's mighty deeds." "The [in]visible being of God is made visible in His deeds, through which He also speaks."

The rare exceptions in the Middle Ages or in Dura Europos (today's Syria) show symbols, but never a divine image. All around Israel figurative images were made. To render divine emanations in human form was normal both to the Greeks and Egyptians. The Hebrews' stubborn refusal ever to give their God any kind of human form not only met with incomprehension among the neighboring peoples, but also led to isolation in trade and cultural exchange. For this very reason, it points to a notable self-awareness founded in God's guidance. There was also another, psychological, aspect to it: When an image does not exist, then an image (that is, a real presence, according to the understanding of the times) is not there to be destroyed. Thus the God of the Hebrews became unassailable and indestructible.

The Olympian Greek religion eventually succeeded in overcoming the last remnants of an old animal cult and the influences of the Thracian cult of Dionysos, although it retained an awareness of the need for a counterpart to the resplendent, harmonious, moderate Being-nature of Apollo. This religion "attained the apex of its greatness in Homer." Occasionally Homer portrays the gods quite humanly, but the boundary between god and humankind is never crossed, or, if so, it is to be punished as hubris, the original sin.

To Plato, God is both personal and impersonal. In Plato's speeches and reflections, the concept of a personal God appears as the highest Idea of the Good, the True, and the Beautiful, and when he is personally involved Plato speaks to God or prays to him. Thus we learn in the *Timaeus*: "The Ideas belong not to the world of experience, but to eternity, although it is only experience that awakens in us an intimation of them. When the human being sees the Ideas in his mind, he makes a connection with eternity." The teaching of the Eastern Church that a real presence lives in icons is based on Plato, for whom the image was not

a mere image of a visible object or person, but was a manifestation of Being.

## TIME AND SPACE

The Greeks know past, present, and future as the three realms
of time. It is a picture of time that we share with them, one in
which the spatial conception wins out over the temporal. The
Hebrews know a past and a present-future, in which the future
is expressed with the present tense of the verb—just as it can be
in German [and English, too—*transl.*] (for example, "She comes
the day after tomorrow.").

The Hebrews picture life as a journey marked by the different events in their personal lives and the life of their people.

Like the Greeks, we say the past lies behind us and the future
before us. "The future may lie before us, but it only arrives
after us." From the psychological point of view, which is that of
the Hebrews, it appears false to say we have the past behind us
and the future in front of us. Actually the reverse it true: the
past lies before us, like an open book. Everything that human
beings have created, formed, built, experienced, and suffered
lies there open to view, while the future lies in the dark. To this
day the Hebrews feel a psychological need, an existential desire,
to read the book of history as a book of life.

In history class, at school celebrations, and other occasions,
to this day Jewish children are to recall the story of God and
His people. This is part of the educational program. The
important thing here is that while learning to know historical
events as thoroughly as possible, the children are actually learning to experience simultaneity, that is, that an event of today
can be linked experientially and emotionally with a similar one
of earlier times. In other words, the crucial thing is that a "psychological reality of those days can coincide with one from the
present, so that an identity" arises through personal involvement, psychologically speaking. Living in the present time connects me with all other living beings.

The Greeks understood time primarily as physical time, which passes and need not be related to events. In the *Timaeus*, Plato speaks of time here below as the "mobile image of eternity." Thus to him, eternity is a condition, a state of being in unmoving rest, without decay, beyond the "gnawing tooth of time." To the Greeks, time was marked by decay, aging, passing. The theorems of geometry and the insights derived from them were not subject to time. They belonged to space and were indestructible, outlasting time. This explains a certain disdain for time on the part of the Greeks. The Hebrews' psychological view of time does more justice to the human being, being more suited to human experience.

While many other peoples oriented themselves by the sun, "the Hebrews oriented themselves by the phases of the moon, by the dependable alternation of day and night, light and dark." The seasons, too, are ever recurring rhythms. "The life of human beings runs in rhythms: earth—man—earth; they pictured the cycle as an eternal rhythm" in which the possibility of a rebirth was not excluded. Yet rebirth never became a central dogma among the Jews. It did not become the plaything for all kinds of speculation. Similarly, as we see in the Book of Job or in the story of the man born blind in the Gospel of John, it was foreign to Judaism to think of karma in terms of personal salvation. Job says: "The Lord gave, and the Lord hath taken away; blessed be the name of the Lord."

Still, this theme is not without its significance. Martin Buber's book *Zwei Glaubensweisen* (*"Two Ways of Faith"*) ends with this remarkable sentence: "An Israel striving for renewal of its faith through the rebirth of the person, and a Christianity striving for renewal of its faith through rebirth of the peoples, would have things untold to tell each other and could render help to one another of a kind scarcely imaginable today!"[2]

Both religions believe in a life after death. The Greeks speak

---

2. Martin Buber, *Two Ways of Faith*, p. 185.

of the immortality of the soul, the Hebrews of the resurrection of the human being.

For the Greeks, the natural way of thinking was spatial. Being concerned with form, it was natural, too, that they attained great accomplishments in geometry and mathematics. It was no problem for them to represent irrational quantities geometrically. They were the great logicians. "Their thinking is synthetic-architectonic. The Hebrew language has no expression at all for the simplest geometric forms— triangle, rectangle, square, and so on. These did not interest them."

The thought of the Hebrews flees logical construction; it is similar to the character of music, in which a theme is continually shaped in new variations.

## GOD'S RELATION TO THE WORLD

For the Greeks and the Hebrews alike, the category of transparency applies to God; that is, God expresses His being in a special manner through the world. He is not only in and above the world. For the Greeks, the Ideas, images, and the symbolic capacity of the world play a significant role. For the Hebrews, the world [is] the instrument with which God carries out his work. Accordingly, one could call the relation of God to the world one of instrumentality. To put this in the Greek manner would be to say that his Being lights up in the world; the things of the world have a symbolic character.

The idea that God was in the person of Jesus Christ and manifested his being through him is conceived in the Greek way; that he sent his son (*logos-dabhar*: the deed-empowered word) and realized his will through him, is thought the Hebrew way. Things became problematic at such moments as when Paul sought to convey Christianity to the Greeks in Israelite thoughts and found no adequate words for them.

For the Greeks, God had a more deductive coloration; furthermore, God lived in Being. The God of the Hebrews lives in history with his people; the Torah and the law give instructions regulating the entirety of life in the 613 commandments and prohibitions. No one, however, watches over these regulations—that is a matter between each person and his or her God. For the Hebrew, having a feeling of God was the criterion by which faith was linked to action. For the Greeks, God is more of a conceptual, ontological idea, and does not necessarily connect with the little matters of everyday life.

### THE TRUE — WHAT IS TRUTH?

The Greeks are eye-people, aesthetes. Plato was characterized as a man of the sense of sight. Just as important as the outer eye was the inner, which was capable of envisioning an idea and of perceiving a spatial or geometric truth. The Hebrews are ear-people; the examples of it in the Old Testament are without number. Whatever we take in through our ears challenges and promotes our inner mobility and wakefulness. If I wish to see something, I must turn my head; and if I wish to look at something else, I must turn my head again. The ears allow everything in, almost without my own permission or activity; and it constantly changes. Ear-people are people of communication, of conversation. Seeing and contemplating can well be the occupation of an individual.

For the Greeks, the True is αλετηεσ—that which is not masked or covered. Being is true and the Good is true. The Hebrews do not ask after an objective Truth. God alone is true. For human beings there are only various approaches to this divine truth. Meaningful things approach the truth, not that which is in agreement with impersonal objective Being. In seeking the truth of a matter, the Hebrew distinguishes the essential from the nonessential in order to get at the core of the matter most directly. Logical proofs and conceptual constructions appear useless to this approach, if the essence of the matter is already visible.

## APPROACHING THE TRUTH THOUGH
## PARABLE AND MIDRASH

Both the Old and New Testaments are positively swarming with parables. One may recall Nathan, who catches David with a simple parable. The trick is that when someone begins telling me a parable, I do not know at first where it is leading and I listen openly. In this way the teller of the parable adroitly gets around my quite understandable justifications and defense mechanisms. Thus I am unprepared when the point of the story—its truth—strikes me, and it hits the bull's-eye.

We see this as well in the parables that Jesus tells the group of fundamentalist Pharisees. Greek thinking is logical and discursive; Hebrew thinking is analytical, understanding through psychological intuition, plumbing the depths.

In our times—certainly due in part to the women's movement and the New Age—there is a new appreciation of "emotional intelligence." Thus today we have access to different kinds of thinking and recognize that all of them together help us experience the reality of our lives better.

## LANGUAGE — DIALECTIC

The Hebrews did not have abstract concepts at their disposal. Frequently they derived these from concrete things that could be seen. The beginning of the human being (seen from the top down) is the head. The word for head is *rosh*. *Rosh* is one of the roots that gives rise to a great many other words, and it means "beginning." *Rosh ha Shana* is the New Year (literally, "head of the year"). The first sentence in the Old Testament ("In the beginning God created the heavens and the earth") begins: *Bereshit bara elohim*. In "reshit" the root *rosh* is hidden.

Greek thinking is oriented not only spatially, but also dialectically, and for this reason it is particularly suited to the areas of science and research.

Hebrew thinking is more oriented toward and related to the human being. Its psychological approach makes it more suited to the realm of ethics and morality, in which the Jews have been trailblazers among all peoples. In their study of Torah the Jews have never known a dialectic of the kind: thesis, antithesis, synthesis. These three steps were perfectly natural to Plato and the Socratics, and have remained so for us. In the study of Torah, synthesis is consciously not sought. In the Talmud, the commentary on the Mishnah (the oral Torah), there will be one opinion and right next to it a contradictory one that is held equally valid. As the saying goes, when there are ten Jews together, there will be twelve different opinions.

Schoolchildren learn early that everything has two sides, that everything is ambivalent. There is not just one single truth, though we are justified in hoping to come closer to truth. This also means that in the thought and teaching of this system, no dogmas exist. Individuals feel called upon to use their own reason, not to subordinate themselves to an official tradition of faith and doctrine. Although decisions are reached by majority, the opinion of the minority remains valid. It need not agree with the majority opinion, though it must acknowledge it.

Since time immemorial, study of the Torah (which is also the basis of law, as there is no state law in our sense) has been a schooling of the mind that goes beyond handing down articles of faith. It helps preserve the mind from prejudices and preconceived opinions, demanding and thus cultivating mobility of soul.

Sigmund Freud writes: "I soon also recognized that I had only my Jewish nature to thank for two qualities that had become indispensable to me on my arduous path in life. Because I was a Jew, I found myself free of many prejudices that limit others in the use of their intellect; as a Jew I had been prepared to go into the opposition and do without the agreement of the 'compact majority'!"[3]

---

3. Rachel Salamander, ed., *Jüdische Welt von gestern*, Vienna 1990, p. 249.

## Two Examples from Stories of the Hasidim

Two Jews come to a rabbi about a legal dispute. The first explains the case: "Rabbi, there is an apple tree growing in my garden. One of its branches hangs over into my neighbor's garden. But the tree is mine, so the apples belong to me too." "You are right," says the Rabbi. The neighbor does not see it the same way, however: "Rabbi, the tree belongs to him, he is right about that, but the apples that hang over into my garden must be my apples." "You are right," says the rabbi.

A student has been paying close attention to the dispute and the decision. Now he says with astonishment: "Rabbi, first you tell one he is right and then you tell the other he is right. Two people cannot both be right in a dispute, can they?" And the rabbi says: "You are right, too."

A Christian farmer in a Polish village admired the cleverness of the rabbi and asked him for advice one day. "The old walnut tree in front of my house was struck by lightning. I don't have the heart to make firewood out of that beautiful tree. What should I do with it?"

The rabbi advised the farmer to have the wood of the tree carved into an image of his patron saint and set it up where the tree had stood. The farmer liked the advice. Soon a statue of the saint stood in front of his house, and all passersby doffed their hats reverentially. Except the rabbi. This irked the farmer and he confronted the rabbi. "Dear friend," said the rabbi, "there is no need to get upset. Why should I take off my hat to him? After all, I knew him when he was still a tree!"

## Shabbat — Torah — Law

As is so often the case, the unique characteristics that arise among the different peoples (among the Jews: the injunctions, the emphasis on doing) have to do with the peculiarities of those they arose among. The Hebrews—always doing, always on their way, always in movement, concerned with changing and improving things—needed a day of rest. Often and quite early on, the Sabbath was personified. On its eve it was welcomed as the long-awaited bride, as a princess, or even—as in Abraham Joshua Heschel—compared to a cathedral. To the Greeks, who were oriented toward vision, including inner vision of ideas and contemplation, and whose idea of the highest state was to rest in divine Being, a specially appointed day of rest was hardly needed. Even today, the majesty and visual splendor of Orthodox services—still often hours long— correspond to a Greek ideal and meet a Greek need.

Shabbat—Torah—the Law: In their diaspora, in the ghettos, wherever they could, the Jews held on to these pillars of their faith and were in turn held by them. Of course, clinging to the law in life can also lead to excesses that are then directed against life, turning into mercilessness, as Jesus revealed in certain Pharisees. The law becomes shallow and misses its purpose.

Excesses in the ideal realm of beauty also arose among the Greeks, especially in the Hellenistic period. In Ephesus, for example, stands a temple dedicated to Hadrian. Or rather, the facade of a temple stands there: the temple was conceived as a facade alone.

## The Constantinian Turning Point

After the Constantinian turning point, when across-the-board Christianizing of the West began, the Greek-Hellenistic approach gained precedence over Hebrew-Hellenistic thinking. Doubtless, power politics played a crucial role in this. Greek thinking had structure, dialectic. There was experience in the development of the *polis*, the structuring of a state. The static, bureaucratic approach to action was more conducive to large-scale Christianization and control. The model of the Roman senate was the one followed. Thus it happened that the Hebrew manner of thinking, with its open, non-dualistic approach and dynamic understanding of God, was largely ignored in the development of the Christian West. Today we are painfully aware that we are missing something critical; many are turning to the East and to Buddhism.

## THE OUTLOOK

In many realms of life today, a symbiosis of Greek and Hebrew thinking has been reached; they live with and alongside of one another in harmony or harmonious contrast: exploration of the world—exploration of the human being. It is no accident that we owe the breakthrough of psychoanalysis to a Jew or that, as is well known, there are a disproportionately large number of Jewish Nobel prize winners.

Our ideal of beauty—in the realm of art and painting, for example—bore a very Greek stamp for millennia, but now it is beginning to integrate the Hebrew approach. The demand that art should elevate, edify, comfort, and surround me with warmth like a relaxing armchair has long since been broken. The abstract artists challenge us. They ask what is behind things; they want to unmask, make a point, dethrone time-honored standards. After all, what mattered to the Hebrews was the statement intended: the content, not the form.

Even today one rarely finds purely beautiful architecture in Israel—and this is not just because of tight budgets. The main thing is that people should have somewhere to live; and if the pragmatic, functional building is beautiful as well, so much the better. Beauty happened to result then; in most cases it was not the primary concern.

In Benedictine monasteries people live by the motto *ora et labora*. Here the two approaches to life are united harmoniously: contemplation and purpose in the world, though so far the latter is almost exclusively the province of men.

The static ontology embodied in the Catholic Church, based on the "Surrogate of Christ" principle of Greek stamp, is highly in need of correction. The immobility and rigidity of church institutions stem from an image of God like the one expressed in the priests' prayers at the canonical hours, in the Hymn of Nones:

*Du starker Gott,*
*der diese Welt im Innersten zusammenhält.*
*Du Angelpunkt,*
*der unbewegt den Wandel aller Zeiten traegt.*

Thou mighty God,
who holds this world together in its inmost being.
Thou fulcrum
who bears unmoved the changes of all ages.

Perhaps in the minds of many Christians the needed correction has in fact taken place, yet the world continues to have a dualistic feeling to it: heaven and God above; we below. God plays too small a role in the little things of everyday life. In our so-called edifice of faith (an image typical of Greek thought) there is no longer any room for the Hebrew approach of open nonjudgment, of letting contradictions stand unreconciled, of a dynamic understanding of God, of a God who lives with his people in history.

To this day Jews speak and argue with their God and their deceased—even in cemeteries—and mourn and pray at the Western Wall. God is with them in the cowshed as naturally as he was for Meister Eckhart.

When the air in our world was heavy with the question, "Where was God when Auschwitz happened?," the renowned Jewish philosopher of religion Abraham Joshua Heschel was one of the first to respond with the answer: "God was in Auschwitz, too." A God without compassion was inconceivable to him, as it is to Elie Wiesel.

Though still dispersed to the four winds, and in spite of all its different movements from ultra-Orthodox to Reform Judaism, the Jewish world has suffered no loss in the substance of its faith. It lives on without a hierarchy, without dogmas, without an official doctrinal center, "office of St. Peter," or congregation of the faithful, and so on. In view of this, as Christians we must ask ourselves if the institutional claim to power, in connection with centralism, is not doing more harm than good.

This attempt to outline the contrasts between the Hebrew and Greek approaches to reality is only a first step. Yet it could prove useful in bringing to life again an interrupted conversation.

The Hasidic Master, Levi Yitzak of Beeditcher, called over a tailor and asked him to relate his argument with God on the day before.

The tailor said: "I declared to God: You wish me to repent of my sins, but I have committed only minor offenses: I may have kept leftover cloth, or I may have eaten in a non-Jewish home, or worked without washing my hands.

"But you, O Lord, have committed grievous sins; You have taken away babies from their mothers and mothers from their babies. Let us be quits: You forgive me and I will forgive you."

Said Levi Yitzak: "Why did you let God off so easily? You might have forced him to redeem all of Israel."

(From Anson Laytner, *Arguing with God—A Jewish Tradition*)

4

# The Blessing

## by Schmuel Hugo Bergman

*from* Info3, *June 2000*

*translated by Magdalene Jaeckel*

*In 1968 the Jewish philosopher Schmuel Hugo Bergman gave the following radio talk over the Südwestfunk Stuttgart. Published in 1993, on the occasion of the twenty-fifth anniversary of the philosopher's death, it has lost nothing of its relevance over the years. Bergman touches here on the question of life's meaning, out of his deep religiosity. While drawing from Jewish sources, he compares them with traditional philosophical schools.*

One of the characteristics of Jewish religious life is the great variety of "blessings." The life of a Jew, be it in daily life or within the synagogue, is permeated by these blessings (Hebrew: *b'rachot*). A Jew's every waking hour, beginning in the morning when he speaks the blessing over washing his hands, until bedtime when he speaks: "Blessed be thou who lettest the veils of sleep fall over my eyes," is filled with these blessings. He speaks them when breaking bread; when drinking; when eating a piece of fruit; at the sight of a rainbow over the ocean; for thunder and lightning; when meeting a wise man; at the occasion of a government official driving by; at the first sight of blossoming trees in the spring; when putting on a new garment; at the news of a friend's death; when meeting an old friend whom he hasn't seen for a year; at being saved from a danger; when perceiving a pleasant fragrance; and, of course, with every religious ritual—for instance, donning the prayer mantle. One can go on and on. The number of these prayers can easily amount to a hundred each day. This means at least eight blessings every waking hour—to think of God eight times every hour!

In some houses of prayer in Jerusalem, mornings after the Sabbath service one can observe a beautiful custom: One community member, often a child, stands by the door and hands those emerging from the house a fragrant flowering branch with one hand, and a piece of fruit with the other. Together they speak the blessings: "To him who has created all the different spices" and "To him who gives fragrance to the fruits." The custom is explained this way: Since the Sabbath prayer only contains seven blessings, as opposed to many more blessings spoken on an ordinary day, one wants to augment the number of blessings in this way.

## MORE THAN GRATITUDE

What is the meaning of these *b'rachot*? The root of the word means: to fall on your knees, to praise and thank God. Hermann Cohen, in *The Religion of Reason, from the Sources of Judaism* writes: "All blessings are a variation of gratitude." We would like to suggest that the meaning of the *b'rachot* is more than that. The dying Jacob "blessed" his grandchildren. The wording of this blessing is still the same today when the father of the family blesses his children at the dawn of the Sabbath day. What does this blessing mean? It couldn't mean that the father "thanks" his children. There has to be an additional meaning in the root *barech*. The father who lays his hands on his son's head in blessing obviously wants to give him something. When we bless someone we want to convey a power, a strength to them, want to let something stream from us into them. The use of this word becomes very clear when we hear at the end of the creation story: "And God blessed the seventh day and made it holy." God added something to the seventh day that made it holy and distinguished it from all the other days. The Jewish interpreters agree: such a blessing means that something good is being added, a spiritual power. In another famous passage, Isaac reveals to Esau that Jacob had "given away" his blessing. Esau calls out: "Twice you have betrayed me now: first you took away my firstborn right, and now you have also taken my blessing from me!" When he then asks his father: "Haven't you saved a blessing for me?" (Gen 27:34-38) we can assume that here also the blessing has more than just a symbolic meaning. It constitutes something concrete that Jacob has taken away from Esau.

In the verses of the fourth book of Moses (Numbers) it is said of the priests: "They shall give my name to the sons of Israel, but I will bless them." The priests can only prepare for the blessing by speaking the required formulas. God himself gives the actual blessing.

If blessing means more than just "saying thanks," we must ask ourselves whether this also applies to the blessings that ordinary people recite? Can we also impart something to one another by saying such a blessing? Or do we have to forget the original meaning when we speak our daily little b'rachot? The always repeated formula is: "Blessed be Thou, O Lord, our God, king of the universe, who has created...." There is a rapid change from the "thou" of the second person to the "who" of the third person, from the God close by to the God above all. Should the significance of the b'racha be confined to a mere "thank you," or do we not have the responsibility to try and adhere to the deeper meaning of this blessing: to convey a strength? This is the question we ask ourselves.

## PARTICIPATING IN THE CREATIVE PROCESS

In one of the most beautiful passages of the Talmud, God himself asks Rabbi Ismael for his blessing: "Ismael, my son, bless me." One of the spokesmen for the German Orthodox

Jews in the beginning of the twentieth century, Jacob Rosen-
heim, has said: "This *b'rachot* expresses a new relationship
between God and humanity. God wants something to happen
on the earth, wants to see a great project prosper that will
unfold over the course of time. To consciously further God's
work on Earth, to participate in the realization of his intention, means to bless God."

Consequently, the meaning of the *b'rachot* must be that it ele-
vates human activity, be it only that of drinking some water or
a glass of wine, to participation in the divine intentions for
the earth, participation in its "redemption." The earthly has
been severed from its divine origin; not the earthly itself, but
our relationship to it. We lose ourselves constantly in our
mundane activities, and thereby we alienate not only ourselves,
but also the things of this world, from the divine origin. They
become, to speak with Heidegger, "Merely godless, material
things." By saying the *b'rachot* we return the things and activities
to their original sacred order, to their divine origin. The Jewish ritual even ascribes a *b'rachot* to the "lowly" activity of elim-
ination. Every function of the body is included in the
sacredness of creation. In contrast to this I mention the attitude of the late Greek philosopher Plotinus. He was ashamed
to have to live in a body. The Jew does not believe that anything material is shameful. It only needs, as does everything in
this world, to be blessed. Therefore Rabbi Akiba says: "Man
is forbidden to use anything of this earth before he has spoken
the *b'rachot* over it." Even though God has given the earth to
humanity, we are not truly entitled to it unless we bless it
every day.

How is this? Is only the human being entitled to facilitate
the return of the earthly to its divine origin? Perhaps nature
also has a part to play in this. We find an answer to this question in one of the lesser-known chapters in the Jewish prayer-
books, "Avodath Israel." Here we find six pages of blessings
that come from the natural phenomena themselves, such as

heaven and earth; day and night; sun, moon, and stars; the clouds, the lightning; wind, dew and rain; the water, the fountains, the rivers, and the sea. These, themselves, speak blessings, and so do the plants, the different sorts of grains, the trees, and finally, the animals. There is a blessing for each of them from the lowliest to the grandest.

While for humanity it is a commandment to say the blessings, the verses spoken by plants and animals are taken from beautiful Biblical passages that describe in poetic words what is being said. The snake, for instance, expresses hope that it will be redeemed from the curse that was laid upon it after Adam and Eve's expulsion from Paradise. It cites the verse from Psalm 145: "He holds up all who have fallen, he helps to straighten all who are stooping down in despair." This whole chapter, called *Perek Schirah*, is filled with humor, light, and deep piety.

### VICTORY OF THE GOOD

How great the contrast between the philosopher Descartes, the "father of modern philosophy," who sees all of nature, including the animals, as machines—as automatons ruled and manipulated by human beings in a dead world—to the prayerful human who hears the whole creation singing its praise to God "with brother spheres, a rival air." Here even hell itself speaks its *b'rachot* when it says the verse from Psalm 107: "They shall say thanks to him for his goodness, for the miracles he does for the children of humanity. He comforts the fainting soul, he fills the hungry soul with goodness."

Even hell believes in the eventual victory of the good, in the redemption of the earth. It seem to me that the decisive question for Jews and all other people is this: Can we, in spite of all suffering, all concentration camps, gas chambers, hydrogen bombs, in spite of all this, have the strength to believe in the final victory of the good, and thereby help to bring it about?

# 5

# ANTHROPOSOPHY AND JUDAISM
## WHAT IS THE CONTRIBUTION OF JUDAISM
## TO THE LIFE OF ANTHROPOSOPHY?

BY SHIMON LEVY

*from* NOVALIS *July-August, 1998, and September 1998*
*transcript of a talk, 1995 summer conference, Dornach, Switzerland*

*translated by Mado Spiegler, edited by Fred Paddock*

DEAR FRIENDS,

The Israeli identity is where it all starts for me: the Hebrew language, the feeling for the landscape and the homeland, the social environment. Judaism was the background of my education in the 1950s at my Jerusalem primary school on the edge of the Orthodox Jewish neighborhood. I absorbed anthroposophy growing up in my parents' home. Time would not be sufficient to describe the many-layered relationships and complicated threads that interweave anthroposophy and Judaism, and those two in turn with the background of Israeli society.

In his book *Working with Anthroposophy,*[1] George Kühlewind writes: "A man can only speak for himself, out of his own experience." My lecture will thus emphasize my own experience, rather than academic aspects or syntheses of contents out of Rudolf Steiner's works and their rhetorical connections with other syntheses about Judaism and anthroposophy.

---

1. Anthroposophic Press, Hudson, NY, 1992.

... Judaism is not just a religion: it is a culture, rooted in an ethnic-tribal reality, while sharing aspects of the various cultures with which it interacted over four thousand years of history. (It) is a unique intellectual and mystical culture, and Jewish identity is a somewhat unique kind of national identity... shaped by repeated exiles. Rudolf Steiner himself has made many fascinating statements on Judaism, Abraham, Moses, Solomon, and the complex Judeo-Christian soil, the understanding of which is indispensable as a background to anthroposophy. In the modern era, Jews have made major contributions to European and Western culture and many Jews have been active in every field of the anthroposophic movement, going back to the earliest days. While Rudolf Steiner had great misgivings about the Zionist goal of incarnating Judaism into a nation-state, the fact remains that, from the encounter between Zionism and the destruction of European Jewry by the Holocaust, Israel was born and became a historical reality.

One of my memories is a letter Robert Lissau wrote in 1961 to Schmuel Hugo Bergman, who then gave it to my mother as a documentation of one individual Jew's relationship with anthroposophy. The writer recalled Steiner having said in the course of a discussion, at the time of his lecture series *Occult Physiology* (Prague, 1907) that a time would come when the Jews would again have a mission in relation to the Christ. This statement, somewhat obscure at the time, and mysterious to the writer for many years afterward, remained however "in my whole inner disposition (*Gemüt*) as a (beacon of) hope for my personal striving, to arise again at the time of the Holocaust." The writer was not alone in that first anthroposophical generation; a number of Central European Jews played an active role, spurred on by the nature of the Christ experience and its relationship to Judaism.

This was one Jew's way of describing his way into anthroposophy. My own access to the relationship between anthroposophy and Judaism was gained through a number of texts, going back to the Old Testament; they represent buds in the long line of the development of the "I" in Judaism. This "thing," the I, is at the very center of anthroposophy; it describes a path from the spirit in the human being to the spirit in the cosmos. It is with this in mind that I am reminded of Baron von Münchhausen's famous story—for many a Jew did just like the Baron, attempted to pull himself out of the marsh of materialism by his own hair. It is to this spiritual pulling oneself out of the marsh that Steiner's *Philosophy of Freedom*[2] is dedicated.

Beyond the fact that we all come from religious, semi-religious or anti-religious backgrounds, there now looms a veritable pseudo-religion, the ever-widening spread of electronic media.... In the age of computers and computer games, video clips and virtual reality, even television and cable-nets are almost as old-hat as are synagogues, temples, churches, mosques and ashrams.... Walter Benjamin had already pointed out the qualitative difference of artworks in the age of reproduction. Endless reproduction, the most important component of the computer age, is a kind of magic, described by Steiner as ahrimanic magic.

At a time when Jewish and Muslim extremists hold each other hostage in the land that has seen the birth of Judaism, Christianity, and Islam, we may well ask: what kind of "information" are we waiting for? Among other questions, there is that of the complex and deep connections between the fundamental truths of Eastern and Western religions, and of the difficult new path proposed by Rudolf Steiner: a path to true spirituality through individual human consciousness experienced in the personal "I."

Yahweh is the God of the "I." When God reveals himself to Moses out of the burning bush, God is identified as "I Am Who I Am" (Exodus 3,14). The Ten Commandments begin with the statement "I, Yahweh am your God," which in Hebrew can *also* be read and understood as "The I is your God," which isn't exactly the same as the divinity introducing itself in the first person!

---

2. Available as *Intuitive Thinking as a Spiritual Path*, Anthroposophic Press, 1995.

In the whole realm of language, there is only one name that in its every essence is distinct from all other names: It is the name "I." All other names can be attributed by the speaker to a thing or a person. The "I" only has meaning when it is applied by a being to the being's own self. The essence of the "I" is independent of all externals; no external force can call me by that name.... "I" is the God's unspeakable name. This is where the soul is holy: that only a being who is of the same nature as the soul can have access to it. God, residing in the human being, speaks when the soul recognizes itself as an "I."

—Rudolf Steiner, *Outline of Occult Science* (1976)[3]

These words are expressed wonderfully in the story of Samuel's prophetic initiation. Samuel is the only man in the whole Old Testament whose birth as well as his death was predicted by a woman seer. He has an interesting biography, which did not always make him a very likable individual among his contemporaries. In the Bar-Mitzvah, the confirmation that he undertook, God himself is revealed. Does he do that out of the soul of the boy whose name signifies "his name is God"?

And the child Samuel served the Lord under Eli. And the word of the Lord was precious in those days; for there was no vision.

And it came to pass when Eli was laid down at his place and his eyes began to wax dim, and he could not see;

And before the lamp of God went out in the temple where the ark of God was, and Samuel was lying down, and asleep;

And the Lord called Samuel, and he answered, Here am I!

And he ran unto Eli, and said, Here am I; for you have called me. And he said I called not; lie down again. And he went and lay down.

---

3. Available as *An Outline of Esoteric Science*, Anthroposophic Press, 1997.

And the Lord called again in the night, Samuel. And Samuel arose and ran to Eli and said, Here am I, for you called me. And he answered, I called you not, my son; lie down again.

Now Samuel did not yet know the Lord, nor was the word of the Lord revealed to him.

And the Lord called Samuel yet a third time. And he arose and went to Eli and said, Here am I, for you called me. And Eli perceived that the Lord had called the boy.

Therefore he said to Samuel, Go, lie down: and it shall be so, if he calls you, you shall say, Speak, Lord, for thy Servant hears. So Samuel went and lay down.

And the Lord came, and stood and called as at other times, Samuel, Samuel. Then Samuel answered, Speak; for thy servant hears.—I. Sam.3, I-IO

Names are very important in this intense initiation story. Over the course of ten verses, God's name is mentioned thirteen times, Samuel's twelve times, and the high priest Eli's seven times—numbers that themselves have well-known magic value since highest antiquity. The text also contains many highly "charged," verbs. Those that apply to Eli are mostly in a negative form or describe weaknesses. Samuel's verbs are exceptionally active ones. He arises, he comes, he goes, he lies down. As far as the characters of the story are concerned, we learn early on that the priest Eli failed in raising his own biological sons, and was being punished as a result. But he succeeded in raising his spiritual son. (This is one of the cases in Jewish history that Steiner mentions in *The Gospel of St. Matthew*[4] where God shifted bloodlines whenever there was a need for human consciousness to take a firm hold: Abraham's successor is Isaac, not his first born Ishmael. It is Esau, not Jacob, who wins the elder son's rights. It is not Reuben but Judah who leads his brothers. Samuel, not Eli's

---

4. Available as *According to Matthew*, Anthroposophic Press, 2003.

biological son, is his spiritual son and the heir of his sovereignty. King David is the descendant of the Moabite woman Ruth.)

The dramatic tension between Yahweh-God, Eli, and Samuel has complex physical, soul, and spiritual aspects. When the story starts, God's candle is still burning, but without the presence of the person called by God, it will be extinguished. God calls insistently, as if God's revelation was as important to him as to human beings. Eli, we are told, no longer *sees*, and we are not just talking about his failing eyesight, but about his spiritual vision, which he is losing or has lost. Samuel, on the other hand, does not yet have the gift. It is in the gap between what used to be and what will be that God calls Samuel to his service, causing an intense dialogue, the beginning of what will be for Samuel a life-long conversation. By contrast, Eli's lack of contact with God is particularly striking. He knows *about* things, from the outside. God's "I" is no longer perceptible to his "I." Samuel's first answer *"Hineni"* (i-e-i) is the key word, meaning "I am here!" Having stated his willingness to serve Eli, he is told that he will have to serve God directly, not by proxy. Ultimately, Samuel will have discovered the God within, in his own name, his own "I."

This "I am here" in response to God is characteristic of the spirit of the Mishnah and the Talmud, the collection of legal discussions, stories, and mystical content that are the fruit of intellectual work as well as enormous ardor. In practice, much more strongly than from the Bible itself, today's Judaism has been formed from the spirit of *Halachah* (the Law), that is the many-branched and unbroken exegesis going on unceasingly since the time of the Talmud. Religious Jews "responded to the call" to action rather than being asked, as in Catholicism, to believe religious dogma. Although the law comes from God, from God's calling, ultimately it is human beings who decide, human beings who respond.

In a telling Talmudic story, one scholar whose opinion was not accepted by the others called upon the heavens to help him. Suddenly, water started running uphill, a tree jumped from one side of the path to the other, and a voice came down from the sky, agreeing with the scholar. Yet his opponents' reaction to this mystical intervention from the spiritual world was to point out that "the Torah has been given to man, it doesn't lie in the heavens." The answers lie in the person's own individuality, and speech is a principal means by which this individuality reveals itself to itself.

The Passover Seder celebration turns around a central act: the reading aloud, the "performance," of the *Haggadah*,[5] a many-layered collage of texts turning around the Jews' departure from slavery in Egypt. More than just a story in which the listener identifies with the passage from slavery to freedom, the telling itself is the ritual, a veritable act of initiation. In the speaking of the *Haggadah*, the "I" goes through a transformation . . . not a transubstantiation of matter (as in the case of the Catholic consecration of the bread and wine) but a "transtemporalization," a jump through time, in which the human being, in the act of speaking, liberates him/herself from bondage. The act is rooted in the human will to break through to a higher consciousness and presence in the world, beyond time- and space-bound daily consciousness.

## KABBALAH AND THE CREATIVE WORD

While they stem from a much older tradition, the classic kabbalistic texts that were such a deep influence on the Theosophical movement and European intellectual life in general were written down in the Middle Ages, at a time when the Kabbalists as a distinct mystical group were especially active in Spain and France, and were in contact with, influenced by, and an influence on Christian and Muslim scholars. One of the best known of them, Abraham Abulafia, was born in Saragossa in 1240 and is known for a rather stormy biography and unsuccessful attempts at a dialogue with the Pope. Aside from

---

5. *Haggadah* actually means "the story."

his certainty that there was no contradiction between mystical inspiration and the sharp rationalism of a Maimonides, his thinking is marked by his insistence on the power of the spoken word. The mystical experience itself, in its highest form, is the process of creating a "text," a process in which experience, exegesis, and performance are indissolubly bound.

In this process, thinking, feeling and willing are all indispensable to the soul's experience of itself in its totality. While this point is taken up by Rudolf Steiner, he differs from Abulafia in his insistence that *every* human being can be creative through speech, whereas Abulafia still felt that it required a particular calling.

Like the old magicians, Abulafia conjures up the divine Wholeness in the sequence of consonants and vowels. It is sounds that guide humans into the spiritual world. Indeed, the members of the human body are assembled like the sounds of speech. The relationship between vowels and consonants is like that between soul and body, each letter like matter, each punctuation like the spirit that weaves through matter. Rudolf Steiner expressed it in similar fashion later, saying that the sounds are the spiritual beings that guide us. In art, in theater, and especially in speech, we bring forth the gods and make visible the soul. If Goethe's Faust comes to mind it is no accident. Abulafia tells of a kind of Faust also, in his story about the magician Joseph de la Rena. While Faust sells his soul to Mephistopheles, Joseph de la Rena is trying to hasten the end of times, the coming of the Messiah, by overcoming two of the chief devils, Samael and Amon of No. If Joseph de la Rena fails in his quest, it is because, having vanquished Samael, he lets him go out of compassion! Like Faust, Abulafia's Jewish magician is pretentious, a little ridiculous, yet also an endearing, if tragically divided, character.

## THE GOLEM

Some Jewish magicians applied their energy to the creation of a human being, to reproduce the act of Genesis. Yet all their attempts failed. Apparently, only a divine being can impart to human beings the "I" that makes them truly human. One very famous story, by Rabbi Loew of Prague, tells of such an attempt in the famous story of the golem, a humanoid being made of clay, assembled by the mere force of a piece of paper on which are inscribed four letters, the unspeakable name of God. While these few letters were enough to create a being, that being, the golem, has no "I," no real humanity. It has no soul, lacks speech and spontaneity, is a silent robot that can only serve the community as a woodcutter and water-carrier, passively doing whatever it is directed to do.

Another story by Gershom Sholem, tells us that the prophet Jeremiah was alone in his reading of the *Book of the Works* (an impossible situation, given the Jewish conception of a book as a necessarily shared, performative experience). He heard a voice telling him: *Seek a friend.* So he went to Sira his son, and together they studied the book for three years. Then they started to assemble the letters of the alphabet using kabbalistic techniques, and behold! There appeared a man on whose forehead stood the words *Yahweh—God is Truth.* But in his hand, the being carried a knife, and with it he mutilated one of the letters, changing the word *Truth* to the word *Dead.* Jeremiah tore his clothes in anguish for now it said *God is Dead* and he asked the golem "why did you mutilate the word?" The creature answered: "Let me tell you a fable. Once upon a time there was an architect who built many houses, towns, and town squares, and no one could compete with his knowledge and skill. But then two men came and convinced him to give them the secret of his art. When they had learned it, they left him and set up shop as architects themselves, and asked only half the price their master had asked. And when people heard about it, they all abandoned the old architect and gave their business to his students." In this way too, God made you in his image. Yet now you yourself try to make a human being and people will say "There is no God besides Jeremiah and his son!" And Jeremiah asked "What shall we do now?" And the creature said: "Write the alphabet on the sand, from end to beginning, without leaving anything out." And when they had done so, the creature fell to dust in front of their eyes.

The story takes place on many levels. It points the reader's attention to the "I." In the story within the story, the created being instructs his creator, the "magician" on the proper way to conduct oneself, and does so at the cost of its own life. The magic thread to Goethe's *homunculus* crosses the spaces between eras and cultures.

## AGNON'S ARCHITECT

There once was an old architect whom the emperor loved, for the palaces, temples, and fortifications he built were more beautiful and distinguished than any other buildings any emperor had ever built. One day, the emperor called him and asked for a new palace to be built. The years passed, and the palace wasn't getting built, for the architect was getting old, and his heart was no longer in the wood and stone. People started pressing him to speed things up. So he took a canvas and painted a palace on it. He made it with great skill, so that everyone thought it was a real palace. He let the emperor know that the palace was ready. And the emperor came and was delighted; it was indeed the most beautiful palace. But someone whispered in the emperor's ear: didn't he see that this was no palace at all, not even the shadow of a palace, just a palace painted on canvas? The emperor was angered. "I elevated you above all other builders, I gave you my entire trust, and this is how you treat me?" The architect was dumbfounded: "What have I done?" And the emperor said: "Now you ask me this ... isn't it enough that you disobeyed my command, betrayed me, and gave me an erasable drawing instead of the real thing?" And the architect replied: "Did you say 'erasable'? We'll see about that!" He knocked with one finger on the painted door, the door opened, and the architect entered the palace and never came out again.

The Israeli writer Shmuel Joseph Agnon, who wrote this story, relates it to a Chinese tradition, and suggests that it has many possible interpretations. One could interpret the palace as God's Torah, which is mere writing into which God—the architect—has entered and now remains invisible. Anyone seeking God would have to enter in the same way, to knock at that door. Many Jewish traditions describe the Scriptures as a veritable spiritual territory, a sea, an orchard, a forest, a rock, a temple.

Modern interpretations might go slightly differently: there once was an old writer, well beloved by the readers of his stories and dramas, but in the end they did not have the trust or the faith to perceive the deeper dimensions of the writer's work. Like Beckett, Handke, or Borges, the writer renounced the hope of communion with his readers and "threw himself into his work." These interpretations and many others are not mutually exclusive—indeed, they complement each other. Agnon, of course, did not invent the architectonic idea of the cosmos. What is emphasized, however, is the relationship between the material temple and the spiritual meaning hidden within it, something that also preoccupied Steiner in his considerations of the relationship between Solomon's temple and the spiritual hierarchies. What is important is that the story demands the reader's involvement, it demands an active, creative participation, not just in understanding the story, but in finding individual, personal meanings. Without the readers' "I," the story does not exist.

Without the boy Samuel's revelation of his "I," he could not have become a prophet. The Passover Haggadah prompts the reader to assert his or her freedom in the act of speaking it. Abulafia the kabbalist showed ways in which speech could be applied and how consciousness is augmented by the potency of the spoken word by which the world was created. Joseph de la Rena, infinitely devoted and compassionate, gave up his soul for an elusive salvation of the world: maybe his "I" was not mature enough, maybe he wanted to hasten his spiritual career and thus destroyed it. Without the cultivation of the "I," what we create is nothing but a "golem," a frightful monster. The story of Agnon's architect is a hermeneutic story, calling upon readers to complete their individual selves in the process of reading it.

Let us finish with a short saying by Rabbi Menachem Mendel from Kutzk: "When I am I, because You are You, then I am not I, and You are not You. Only when I am I, *and* You are You, am I truly I and You truly You."

When Israel, the Rebbe of Rizhyn was asked by his disciples how to serve God, he said, "How should I know?" But he then told this story: Two friends were found guilty of an offense, and the king, who wanted to be merciful, sentenced them to undergo the following ordeal. A rope was strung across a vast cavern; if they could cross on it to the other side they would be free. The first one got safely across, and his terrified colleague yelled across the chasm to find out how he did it. The friend responded, "All I know is that when I felt myself toppling over to one side, I leaned to the other."

(Martin Buber, *Tales of the Hasidim*, bk. 2, "The Later Masters").

# 6

# THE KABBALAH, AN ESOTERIC BRIDGE TO CHRISTIANITY?

## BY ROLF UMBACH

*from* NOVALIS, *June 1997*

*translated and abridged by Mado Spiegler*

### DISCOVERY OF THE KINSHIP OF KABBALAH AND CHRISTIANITY

WHEN Pico della Mirandola (1546-94) published his *Conclusiones*, he launched a discussion that was to have momentous consequences for him. When the Pope rejected his theses as heretical, he fled to France. The Pope's decree followed him there and he was arrested, to be freed thanks only to his relationships with very high nobility; Ludovico de Medici intervened and extended his protection over Pico, allowing him to remain free for the few years left to him.

What exactly had his heresy consisted of? Pico had attempted to make a synopsis of all religions, hoping to prove that Christianity included all religions in itself—or, put differently, that what other religions merely adumbrated was revealed in full clarity in Christianity, or could easily be integrated with Christianity.

Pico had been particularly interested in the Jewish esoteric traditions and had made the astounding discovery that not only did Jews and Christians have the Old Testament in common, as had been accepted till then, but the kinship included theological concepts that had been considered unique to Christianity. As far as he was concerned, such a discovery should, if anything, strengthen Christians' faith, while also awakening the hope that the Jews would realize that they had actually been Christians all along without knowing it, and that simple intellectual honesty would dictate conversion to Christianity.

For Pico to "take over" the Kabbalah, which had been held in high esteem by the Jews as a source of deep and fruitful religiosity, was clearly threatening to the Jewish rabbis, who were not about to encourage their flock in that direction.

As for Christian philosophers, they feared for their monopoly over the truth. They saw the threat of the church becoming a kind of pantheon in which the God of Christian revelation would merely occupy a slightly higher throne, and of other religions no longer being considered garbage to be swept away from in front of the church doors and thrown away in disgust. The faithful were to be warned sternly against Pico della Mirandola's acceptance of the Kabbalah as a source of legitimate knowledge.

On the other hand, the Renaissance brought not just a rebirth of ancient philosophy and its myths, but also quite an interest in antique mysteries that had been repressed by the victory of Christianity and forgotten. Pico della Mirandola's insights pointed to the possibility of a rebirth of the Hebrew mysteries, which had been preserved in the Kabbalah after the diaspora. Further fascination came from the fact that in the Kabbalah one could find parallels to the natural science developed by the alchemists. There, materials were separated through fermentation and burning or cooking and distillation, and sublimated and reconstituted at higher levels, where they acquired their true force and nature. Something very similar happened in the Kabbalah. The Hebrew letters are also numbers, enabling the reader to read each word as a number; that is, to break it down into its constituent elements. According to the old traditions of gematria, one can then search for other words with the same numerical value and different meanings. The shared numeric basis makes it possible to discover the secret connection between words, at a higher level. Gematria thus provided surprising and deep insights into the secret meaning of apparently meaningless passages of a text.

## THE SEPHIROT TRADITION AND ITS ECHOES OF THE TRINITY

The Christian kabbalists were fascinated when they turned to Pico's pioneering work to try and find the hidden meaning in the Old Testament. They made a particularly revolutionary discovery: if one read the Old Testament from the point of view of the Kabbalah, it seemed underpinned by a secret crystalline scaffold in which one could discern representations of the Trinity. This represented such a surprising correspondence with their own mystical inclinations that the Christian kabbalistic scholars proceeded to delve deeper into the secret Jewish teachings. To the church functionaries who looked askance at their work and to skeptical colleagues, they explained away their studies as a preparation for a mission of conversion of the Jews that would be more successful than the earlier ones. In reality, this explanation was merely a cover-up; missionary successes were hardly what the Christian kabbalists were concerned about.

As we pointed out earlier, the connections with the trinitarian teachings were the most attractive part of the Jewish mystical traditions for the Christian kabbalists. They saw in them an early evolutionary stage of Christianity's central dogma that had been integrated in the first two phrases of the Nicene Creed. The question whether perhaps the dogma of the Trinity had its actual origin in the Jewish Kabbalah was foreign to them. But this question cannot be evaded, especially if we want to see, as is the case here, whether the Kabbalah may represent a bridge between Judaism and Christianity.

The teaching of the Sephirot is a central pillar of the kabbalistic system and we will therefore sketch it out here.

The visual representations of the Sephirot are primarily regarded as a support to understanding, and as such we cannot renounce them. But we may note that in the Zohar, the main kabbalistic book, there are no such schematic representations, and even the word *sephirot* is not used, but instead words like "lights, colors, crowns, paths." The discipline of the Arcanum still seems to be at work in the Sephirot teachings that—until the publication of the Zohar at the end of the thirteenth century—had only been transmitted among a circle of trusted companions. After the publication of the Zohar, many interested people could work with it, but without guidance anyone trying to find their way through the labyrinthine work was doomed to get lost.

The word *Sephirot* is the plural of *sephira* (number) and is often referred to as the "Book of Numbers." This, however, does not take us very far, for Sephirot is understood as designating the ten "emanations"—that is, manifestations—of divine power. Creation came out of them and is preserved by them. The burning spark of creation summoned up the Sephirot and eventually brought about the creation of the whole material world. The Kabbalah is foreign to precise philosophical or theological concepts, and so it is never entirely clear whether the Sephirot designate forces created by God or whether they precede the creation, being "witnessed but uncreated." Unlike Dionysios the Aeropagite's nine angelic choirs, the Sephirot are not ordered in a strict linear hierarchy, but rather are represented as a tree with three trunks, in which the kabbalists see the Tree of Life (Genesis 3:22).

It is best to think of that tree as growing upside down, so that the sephira *Kether* represents the root stock out of which the three stems grow. The right-hand trunk is assigned to the masculine force, the left to the feminine force. The middle trunk is the trunk of balance/balancing.

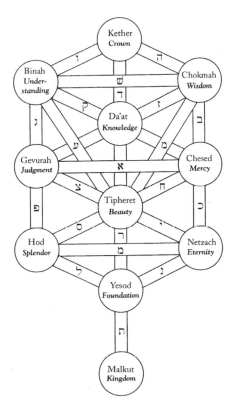

The representation of the Sephirot included six horizontal layers of three elements each. These six triads are crossed by three verticals, so that each of the stems is made up of three parts, a trinity itself. This means that altogether we have nine different combinations of the Trinity.

A schematic presentation of the Sephirot-tree allows six trinitarian coordinates to be recognized:

| | | | | |
|---|---|---|---|---|
| Kether (1) | – | Chokmah (2) | – | Binah (3) |
| Chokmah (2) | – | Binah (3) | – | Tipheret (6) |
| Chesed (4) | – | Gevurah (5) | – | Tipheret (6) |
| Tipheret (6) | – | Netzach (7) | – | Hod (8) |
| Netzach (7) | – | Hod (8) | – | Jesod (9) |
| Netzach (7) | – | Hod (8) | – | Malkut (10) |

To these six triads, three verticals are added. These consist of the trinities of the two outer trunks of the Sephirot tree plus the inner trunk of Kether, Tipheret, and Malkut. With that we have nine trinitarian connections before us. (Yesod is so closely connected to Tipheret that it is considered to be included in that Sephira.)

The outer Sephirot are seen as antipathetic forces, which are balanced by the central trunk, thus avoiding the destruction of the system as the result of an imbalance. *Chesed* and *Gevurah*—compassion and justice—make this particularly clear. Loving, forgiving compassion sets no boundaries, for that would be like trying to contain a river without banks. On the other hand, rigid justice by itself would result in everything drying out, like life in a desert where the rain never falls. In philosophical terms, we find in the Sephirot the pendulum of thesis and antithesis, coming to rest in the synthesis, or as seen by Taoists, Yin and Yang.

*Sepher di-Ziniutha*, the *Book of Hiddenness*, which comes at the beginning of the collection of texts assembled under the title of Zohar, starts with the dark words: "The *Book of Hiddenness* is the book of the balancing of opposites. *Before there was balance, no face could see any other face, and the first kings were dead, their crowns no longer to be found, and the earth was a desert waste.*"

The first kings in the quote above refer to the seven disappeared kings in Genesis 36.31 who, according to kabbalistic tradition, had ruled in a pre-creational world that had since been annihilated. Out of the debris of these annihilated worlds the present world was created, and this one will persist, for it is built on the "scale of balancing," the foundation of the Sephirot—a system of balancing opposites.

The introduction to the *Book of Hiddenness* does not just speak of the balancing of opposites. It also says: "no face could see any other face." This means that the mutual seeing of faces is a mirroring resulting from creation. In this mirror, the world above incarnated (literally, *in-imagined*) itself in the world below, which was thus called into being.

For the Sephirot, the world below means the seven Sephirot below the top triad of *Kether, Chokmah,* and *Binah.* Thus the trinitarian configurations of the lower Sephirot are resonances of the top three. The seven lower trinities are also called the "short-faced one" or son, born from the union of the Father and *Binah,* (also called the higher mother). Whenever Genesis speaks of God as *Elohim,* it means the Kabbalah's *Binah* or *Higher Mother,* from which the creation proceeded in seven days. And the Kabbalah does not read the first words as "In the beginning, God created," but rather "God created Six," meaning the six lower Sephirot from *Chesed* to *Yesod. Malkut,* the tenth and last one, is never included in the count, for it is entirely turned toward humanity and only temporarily connected with the other Sephirot.

*Kether,* the Old One of the Days, is called "the long-faced one," and it is said of him that his face is only visible in profile, the other side remaining forever hidden. This other side of the face is *Ein-Sof,* the Unknowable, to whom *"all-that-is-yet-isn't"* is turned. *Ein-Sof* is beyond experience and beyond words. A paradoxical concept of "negative existence" is the closest thing to it, insofar as *Ein-Sof* is completely alien to any human possibility of understanding it or coming close to it. Thus the Kabbalah considers it downright blasphemous to pray to *Ein-Sof* or ask for its help. All that can be said of *Ein-Sof* is that it is the Urground, the archetypal ground of all that became. *Kether,* the highest sephira, is closest to *Ein-Sof,* and represents it to some extent in the higher reaches of "that which became" (as opposed to "that which was there from all eternity"). In *Kether, Ein-Sof* hid the seed of all that was meant to become.

Just as *Kether* represents the origin of the other sephirot, turned toward them, yet separate, so *Malkut* is related to material creation. She is always near, but the material world has no power over her. Due to her protective, nourishing role toward all creatures, she is called the Lower Mother. She is also the bride of *Tipheret,* and is forever rising toward him to unite with him in love. Depending on context, *Malkut* is sometimes called the *Shekinah*. As *Shekinah* she is the presence of God among humanity, not an abstract presence, but a very concrete one, personified even. When God banned humanity from his presence, she followed them into exile and assumed their fate. This doesn't mean that she is a fallen sephira, but rather that she is the hope and the promise that one day human exile would end and that she would return home with them. *Malkut-Shekinah* clearly has aspects of the Madonna, the mother full of grace. She is also the guardian of the wedding bed. The joy of human love pleases her. In this respect she is different from Mary, from whom earthly colors were bleached out.

The trinitarian aspects of the Kabbalah described above are all drawn from the Sephirot, that is, the *Book of Hiddenness* that introduced the Zohar. But the teaching of the Sephirot is by no means limited to this book. All the writings of the Zohar turn around this occult message. Let us take a look at one of these other interpretations as a bridge to the Trinity.

In Folio 2.136 of the Zohar, we find a mystical interpretation of Psalm 19, verses 3 and 4:

> Day speaks to the other day and Night to the other night—
> without words and without language (Ps. 19:3,4)

which the Zohar explains:

> One day to the other, one level to another, the one to the other to complete and illuminate. "Word" (Hebrew A-M-R) bringing together the signs and the path that come from the father and the mother with the one that proceeds from them, the son, the firstborn. The *Aleph* (A) designates the father; it rises and falls, unites with the *Mem* (M), the word "mother;" the *Resch* (Resch, meaning R, can also be read *Rosh* in Hebrew, and then means *head*) designates the head, the firstborn. From the unity of the three, the Word is

born ... so all things are complete in the Word, who reigns above all things and in it all things are united.

Let us point out that when the Zohar speaks of the days and levels, it means that they reflect for each other the light of the higher realms. Thus illuminated, they become perfect. Father and mother are *Chokmah* and *Binah*, son is *Tipheret.*

In this interpretation of the psalm we encounter the trinitarian configuration of *Chokmah, Binah, and Tipheret*, visible in the signs A-M-R that, when read together, come out as WORD. The Son therefore is the Word.

The association of this Word to the creating Logos of which John speaks at the beginning of his Gospel almost forces us to see here the Son of the New Testament.

We must ask here the reasons for this similarity. It is quite clear that in the cult of the newly developing religion, the common inheritance of the mystery religions and Jewish esotericism is evolving. The secret wisdom of the Sephirot was transmitted by Jewish esotericists who had become Christians in the first centuries. The three upper sephira, which are set slightly apart in traditional versions, would then have been clearly separated and made into the Christian Trinity, the lower ones being turned into angelic choirs.

One could also argue from the same elements that the Kabbalah was influenced by Christianity. But there is very little evidence of this. This could only be conceivable if the Zohar had not for centuries been placed side-by-side with the Torah and the Talmud. Judaism had a finely honed sense for that which was flesh of one's flesh, limb of one's limb: by the thirteenth century (when the Zohar first appeared), the sufferings of the Jews at the hands of Christians had been such that resonances from Christian dogma would almost certainly have met with outraged rejection, and the Zohar condemned. Yet the opposite is the case: the Zohar was greeted with enthusiasm when it had first been placed.

## THE FOURFOLD STRUCTURE OF THE WORLD

But alongside these trinitarian echoes, the Kabbalah also presents notable differences from Christian dogma. One difference appears when we look at the four-part divine name, so important in the Kabbalah: YHWH, which even today is unpronounceable. It was the Christians who added vowels to the consonants, and pronounced it Jehovah or Yahweh.

The fourfold aspects were indicated in the Zohar but were not fully developed until the Kabbalah of Isaac Luria (1534-1572). From the very beginning, the threefold and the fourfold aspects were not opposed but complementary, the whole perspective only becoming visible when both are seen together. The triad and the quartet are related to each other like the numbers three and four. Adding them up gets us to seven, the pleroma, the fullness of being. Multiplying them by each other we get twelve, which encompasses all things in heaven and on Earth, in time and space. Since it is impossible to get to seven or twelve without four, it means that four opens up the full depth of the Trinitarian teaching. Trying to avoid four means maiming the spiritual form of the Kabbalah.

For the Kabbalah, there are four spiritual, immaterial worlds. The highest world is *Aziluth*, out of which flows a stream of light of immaculate purity and infinite energy. This ray of light first goes through a prism in which the colors are divided, while remaining timeless and immaterial. This is the world of the *Be'ia*, the world of creation. In the next stage, the now-divided ray reaches a level where it assumes form, as if it were to pass through a filter in which the outlines of later *gestalts* and events were formed. This happens in the world of forms, *Yezira*. Only then does the ray of light reach the world of *Assiya*, the world of actual material, sensory existence.

In these four worlds, the tetragrammaton is inscribed, that is, the four holy letters YHWH in which the Sephirot meets the teachings about the four worlds.

Reading from right to left, the first letter, the Y (*Yod*), is the smallest letter of the Hebrew alphabet. Its form is reminiscent of a seed, and as a seed it stands for the whole of creation. Thus *Yod* stands for the *Chokmah*, the inseminating father, whose potency is not, however, self-contained. A small point at the top of the *Yod* stands for this power lodged by *Kether* into the *Yod*, thus making *Chokmah* into the seed of all that has and will become. *Yod*'s numerical value is ten; that is, the return of the one, which is the value of *Kether*. In its relation to *Kether*, *Chokmah* is feminine, for only when penetrated by *Kether* does *Chokmah*'s (paternal) potency come into being. But when the sephira *Chokmah* unites with *Binah*, the High Mother, it is masculine.

*Binah* is represented by the letter *H*. The little opening under the top bar, the "window" is a symbol of openness to the instreaming of *Chokmah*'s creative power. As mentioned earlier, the union of *Chokmah* and *Binah* gives birth to *Tipheret*, the Son. *Tipheret* is also the heart, the integrating center of the sephirotic tree. The letter *W* (*Vav*) with a value of six, stands for *Tipheret*. The last letter of the divine name, the second *H* stands for *Malkut*, the tenth and last sephira, mentioned earlier as the Lower Mother.

As far as Kabbalists are concerned, our scientific attempts to derive the names of God from archaic conceptions are devoid of any insight into the real relationships. They know, of course, that next to YHWH, there also exists the name *Elohim*, but whenever the book mentions two divine names, kabbalists see it as a proof of the mysteries of the divine nature, but in no case as an indication of conflicting traditions of the kind biblical scholarship thinks it has identified.

If we return to the tetragrammaton's interpretations, we may note that they only speak of the *spiritual* worlds, not about our material world. Our world is completely identified with the Lower Mother, the mediator and nurturer of the lower world. In theological terms, the divine name YHWH means that human beings never completely lost their place close to—even within—God. They were only temporarily banned, since the fourth letter was never eliminated from God's name. With that it is promised that, at some time, that which God has inscribed with his name and has allowed to remain inscribed will come into true being and the ban on humankind will be lifted.

The two *H*'s in the divine name stand for the two mothers, their signs fused with the masculine letters *Yod* and *Vav* to form an inseparable entity. The tetragrammaton is thus the expression of the balancing of the opposites and of the accomplishment of all things. How can that be? For nothing is completed, the cosmic process is still going on!

In fact, the second *H*, the Lower Mother, is only partially blended with the other three letters, part of it moves away from them. We are thus looking at an ongoing process of suffering, nostalgia, and loving fulfillment reflected on Earth in the love of man and woman. Only when *Malkut* lovingly unites with *Tipheret*, the center of the Sephirot, does her blessing power come to the full, and she needs this blessing power in order to preserve the world. Even though *Malkut* is temporarily separated from her beloved, her sign always remains inscribed in the divine name. Therefore God is both male and female, man and woman. This is reminiscent of the modern discomfort with the idea of a purely masculine Trinity and feminist theologians' efforts to rediscover the feminine side of God in the Holy Spirit. While this may rehabilitate the feminine to some extent, it would in no way lead to the quaternal totality.

Let us note also that for the Kabbalah, the world and humankind are not totally corrupted as they are in Luther, following Paul and Augustine. It is no accident that the Kabbalah speaks of humanity's exile and banishment, not of a fatal curse. For God in the form of the *Shekinah* has followed humankind even into its exile, and remains always near.

This also means that the Kabbalah cannot really integrate the concept of a savior whose blood-sacrifice is necessary to give the world and humanity the necessary forces to overcome the Fall.

Put differently: the form of a savior thus imagined would have to break the divine name, as the kabbalists understood it. If there is anything resembling salvation in the Kabbalah, it is in the image of Sinai. The Kabbalah teaches that when Moses received the written and the spoken Kabbalah there, the way to the Tree of Life was reopened....

The Kabbalah does not doubt in the least that at the end of times, the Messiah—the Christ—will appear, gather his own, and establish the kingdom of God on Earth. This teaching is actually very important, yet the apocalyptic Messiah is not understood as the creating Logos and Savior who had earlier sacrificed his own life. In other words, the figure of Christ is not integrated in the messianic teaching of Judaism.

We had said earlier that the fourfold symbolism in the Kabbalah did not necessarily help build bridges between Judaism and Christianity. At the same time, there are definite parallels insofar as in both religions rational, logical thinking is seen as insufficient, and thinking in images and symbols plays an important role. The kabbalistic and the Christian esoteric worldviews both take as their starting point the existence of higher, immaterial worlds. And, like esoteric Christianity, the Kabbalah also speaks of reincarnation. However, while these may be points of contact, they are not very strong bridges, and there are other points of divergence in the realm of daily life. For Judaism, it is quite clear that the coming of the Messiah-Christ is supposed to involve very concrete material-temporal consequences. Only when the Messiah has unquestionably come will the law be lifted.

But the created world is still in its birth pangs. No perceptible changes took place after the Christian Messiah's coming! The world still needs priests and laws. Would it not be asking for trouble of the worst kind, then, to stop following the law, with its prescriptions aimed at healing and blessing the world? For the kabbalistic Jew, obedience to the law with its innumerable prescriptions and proscriptions is a spiritual practice, an uninterrupted mystical liturgy of daily life. Through it, thinking turns into action and action turns to thinking, without interruption. Yet for Christians, the acknowledgment of Jesus of Nazareth is supposed to mean that the law is lifted, and from a Christian point of view, for anyone to keep practicing the law would be meaningless, a form without function, a symbol cut off from its spiritual root.

Furthermore, for the kabbalist, the Hebrew language is an integral part of spiritual life. In Hebrew, every passage of the Bible has secret overtones whose melody conducts the reader directly to the Sephirot, the mysteries of creation, the presence of God's Shekinah among human beings. Yet the name of the Messiah Jesus does not figure among those overtones. For the Christian, on the other hand, there were no expectations that the first coming of Christ would have physically altered the world. Its reality is primarily of a mystical nature. For esoteric Christianity, on the other hand, the resurrection of Christ has started a gradual transformation in the very earth-processes and cosmic alignments: a belief that makes the building of bridges with kabbalistic Judaism seem far less problematic, the possibility of an esoteric-spiritual community not far-fetched at all, given the many similarities we described earlier.

### THE TEACHING PICTURE OF THE PRINCESS ANTONIA

We will conclude this search with a look at a work in which an imaginal, painterly attempt was made to build just this kind of bridge in the seventeenth century, when there were powerful streams at work (in Central Europe particularly) seeking to build up the links between Christianity and the Kabbalah. The painting was made in 1673 for Princess Antonia of Württemberg, and is still standing in the Church of the Trinity in Bad Teinach. The viewer is led with the seeking soul, a young woman leaning on a cross and anchor (the symbols of faith and hope), before a whole panorama of revelation. The seeking soul is facing Jesus, who stands at the center amid the twelve sons of Jacob. Behind Jesus, a staircase leads to the entrance of the Temple. Above the gate of the Temple, we see a Madonna with the child, and above her a round medallion within a square within a triangle. At the center of the cupola, the Trinity is represented, flanked by the Sephirot, Moses with the burning bush, Elijah with a sword, and Enoch with a book. At the very top, we see the imperial crown and the divine monogram YHWH, surrounded by the twenty-four old men from John's Book of Revelation. Left and right, we see Michael and the dragon and the throngs of the saved on Zion surrounded by angels.

There are many more details; looking at them all, we would see that in this single image are represented all the most meaningful figures of the Old and New Testaments, as well as the main tenets of the Christian faith, together with a few kabbalistic teachings. Certainly also, we must appreciate the quality of the effort that was made here to present the story of salvation as a current event rather than as a past event placed in a linear historical frame. We are far from the scientific rendition of "historical facts." It is, from an artistic point of view, unquestionably successful, and lends itself at first to the feeling that in this beautiful image, the bridge of which we were speaking has indeed been built. Further viewings, however, reveal how little of the Kabbalah has been included. Of course, the Sephirot is there, and so are the square and the triangle and the divine monogram, all pointing to the mysterious nature of God. But in the end, whereas the Kabbalah aims at giving keys to the secret meanings of the Torah and to the gates of Paradise, what we have here are mere "quotes" of figures and events from the Old Testament, seen as projections behind Jesus. All the events of the Old Testament are represented, in very classical Christian fashion, as premonitions of the life and death of Jesus.

One is left wondering: despite her unquestionable goodwill toward the Kabbalah, had the Princess Antonia really transcended the vision of the synagogue that is represented in the

Strasbourg portal, attempting to read the Scripture through
her blindfold? In some way, Princess Antonia's painting still
"reads" the Jewish "text" through the filter of Christianity. All
the elements are there, the words are there, but not the "syntax," and certainly not the hidden syntax that is such an important part of the kabbalistic language.

# 7

# SPIRITUAL BACKGROUND:
# THE COSMIC CHRIST IN JUDAISM

## BY DAVID SCHWEITZER

*from* INFO 3, *June* 2000
*translated by* Mado Spiegler

IT IS COMMONLY *assumed that the differences and opposition between Judaism and Christianity hinge around the concepts of Messiah and Christ. David Schweizer's meticulous comparison of the two ideas provides new elements for research and suggests unexpected convergences, which in turn open new perspectives on anthroposophy. The Hebrew word Messiah or Mashiach means "the anointed." Christ is the Greek word for the same concept. As he endeavors to understand what Christ /Messiah means for Judaism, he briefly recalls Rudolf Steiner's conception of Christ as event.*[1]

## THE CHRIST IN ANTHROPOSOPHY

Briefly put, the word *Christ* or *Christ Impulse* designates the renewal or shoring-up by the creative Logos of fundamental human elements that had been weakened by the combined influences of Lucifer and Ahriman. For this renewal to take place, the Logos, a most holy divine entity, needed to move closer to the human being. Furthermore, it required that the "I" be saved, for the evolution of individual consciousness depends

---

1. Cf. Oskar Kürten, *Der Sonnengeist Christus in der Darstellung Rudolf Steiners* and *Jesus von Nazareth, mit Anhang: Der Menschensohn und der kosmische Christus*, Basel, n.d.

upon the integrity of the physical body: it is the latter that is destined to give birth to the higher spiritual being in the human. In the Mystery of Golgotha, the Logos and earthly humanity came as close together as possible. In Golgotha, the forces of the Logos were most active in the supersensible component of the human being that underlies the physical body.

The Christ impulse is an "I" impulse. At Golgotha, the forces of the cosmic "I" flowed into the earth, to be taken up by the human being through a life of love and spirituality....[2] This event had been prepared by three stages, each with decisive effects upon earthly humanity: the redemption of the astral body, [the redemption of] the etheric body, and [the redemption of] the physical body.[3]

Thus, when Rudolf Steiner speaks of the "Christ," he is talking of several spiritual beings whose collaboration (over time) made this evolution possible. One was the Jesus-Soul, whose virginal, uncorrupted quality was inherent in primordial humanity (Adam Kadmon) before the luciferic influence resulted in the Fall and the expulsion from Paradise. From this original humanity of Adam Kadmon, one part was preserved for the future, watching humankind closely from the spiritual world, participating in its destiny out of love, and redeeming successive parts of the human being. Throughout this process, the Jesus-Soul was host to the pervasive presence of a helping archangel.[4] The archangel entity is one of the entities that Steiner includes under the generic word "Christ."

The first incarnation of that Jesus-Soul was Jesus of Nazareth.[5] The archangelic entity connected with that incarnation is also related to two other Christic entities. The first is the Logos,

---

2. See Kürten, *Jesus von Nazareth*, p. 57; also Rudolf Steiner, GA 155, lecture 3.

3. Kürten, op. cit., p. 16, ff.

4. Kürten, op cit., p. 10 ff.

5. Rudolf Steiner, GA 13, Lect. 10, *Man in the Light of Occultism*, Garber Communications, Blauvelt, NY, 1989.

the divine, creative cosmic Word, active in all Christ-related events. The second is a higher spiritual being, a *light body* whose innermost core is the Logos. The Logos and its *light body* descended from the furthest reaches of the cosmos at the time of the Old Sun, and on that account Rudolf Steiner calls this *light body* of the Logos the "sublime solar spirit Christ," whom the Holy Rishis of old India called *Vishna Karman*, the Zoroastrians *Ahura Mazda*, the ancient Egyptians *Osiris*, and the Greeks *Helios*. On the ancient Sun, the Christ archangel had undergone a phase of human evolution and was the most highly evolved spirit there, and is now the leading spirit of the sun and the "regent" of the solar system, due to its having been suffused by the Logos and united to the sublime solar spirit within which the divine Word, the Logos, was active. "... By identifying with the creative divine element, the ineffable verb, and by the substitution of selfless love for any kind of glory, the Christ... expanded his rulership to all other planets." The sublime solar spirit and the Logos, being cosmic entities, are situated well beyond the reach of the human being and cannot be directly incarnated in a human being. In order for the mystery of Christ to be realized on Golgotha, there thus needed to be an entity closer to the human being, that is, the Christ Archangel.[6]

Rudolf Steiner includes yet other beings under the name of "Christ," for example, the Mystic Lamb, the Cosmic I, and the oneness of the seven Elohim, which the Bible calls YHWH-Elohim.[7] In other words, there are many other auxiliary spiritual components of the Christ event. The Logos is at work behind and through all of them, and they too can be called "Christ."

## THE DIVINE AND ITS NAME—JEWISH MONOTHEISM

Jewish tradition knows several names for the divine being (*Elohim, YHWH, YHWH-Zebaot, Ka'vod,* etc.). All those names ...

6. Kürten, *Der Sonnengeist*, p. 254.

7. Rudolf Steiner, GA 122,*Genesis*, Rudolf Steiner Press, London, 1989.

designate *ways in which God acts in the world; they are forms of the divine relationship with human beings.*

The entities these names designate are inseparable from God (hypostases). "Elohim," for instance, designates the "force that distinguishes and separates." This force appears at several levels of sacred hierarchies, distinguishing different levels of the divine emanation. It is this force that was used by God at the creation of the world to separate light from darkness, solid from liquid, and so on.... This force is an intrinsic part of various entities and acts through them. Thus the gods of Egypt and of other nations, angels, or even human beings (Moses) can all be designated by the name Elohim (Exodus 7:1).

The name YHWH has another meaning. When Moses wants to see God, the latter answers "I will proclaim to you the name of 'YHWH', and will be gracious to whom I will be gracious and will show mercy on whom I will show mercy." ... and further "...The Lord passed before him and proclaimed: YHWH, YHWH, long suffering and slow to anger, abundant in goodness and truth, keeping mercy for a thousand generations, forgiving inequity and transgressions, yet will by no means clear the guilty" (Exodus 33: 19; 34: 6-7).

The name YHWH, by which Moses calls God, signifies the divine activity, full of grace toward the human being but demanding actions in return. The insistence on retribution is a return to the notion of karma, which is as familiar to Jewish mysticism as is the idea of reincarnation. We shall see later how this connects with the Logos.

In his most secret aspects, God cannot be called by *any* name. The more we penetrate into occult, divine dimensions, the less possible it becomes to use a name, for its meaning is no longer accessible to the human mind. Among these designations, before we come to the *Un-namable*, we find the *Ein-Sof* (the infinite) and *Ayin* (*nothing*). "Nothing" as a name of God is mentioned in Exodus 17.7. In that passage, the Israelites "tempt" God by asking Moses who is present among them: "Is it YHWH, or Nothing?" (Standard interpretations, by the way, are misleading, for they have them asking "is God present among us, or isn't he?").

Behind their question, we find the idea that "YHWH" and "Nothing'" were two different gods, rather than being two different *names* for the same God. This mistake had momentous consequences for the people, and resulted in the appearance of the Amalekites—who were human only in their physical appearance, but not in their deeper nature; they were the incarnation of evil, separated from God. With the Amalekites's attack, the Israelites experienced the consequences of this division of the One God into separate gods.

Strict monotheism did not prevent Judaism from recognizing the existence of a very rich spiritual world, filled with immaterial entities at the most diverse levels, and with the most diverse attributes. Judaism had its own hierarchies, from which came the names used in Christian esoteric writings: Cherubim, Seraphim, Michael, Gabriel, Raphael, and Uriel, to mention only a few. Everything that God does in the world is done through the intermediary of spiritual entities. Mainstream Jewish texts call them "angels" (*malak:* messenger) and in line with Aristotle, characterize them as immaterial beings of reason. These intelligences move the cosmos; they rule the becoming and waning of nature. In this respect, they have their own freedom in the exercise of a will analogous to human will, freedom granted them by God through his emanation.[8] When Abraham or one of the Old Testament prophets says that God told him such and such, this generally means that an angel appeared to him.[9] In Exodus 23. 20-21, it is announced to Israel that God will send an angel whom they must listen to, for in him resides the name of God. This means that God's will is being expressed by the angel. Such a divine will using a divine spiritual entity is also called "Word of

8. Maimonides, *Guide for the Perplexed*, 2.7, 10.
9. Maimonides, op. cit., 2 ch. 34, 41.

God."[10] Through the language of "*Word* or *Will* of God, it is the *Logos* that is meant. Jewish monotheism is present in Paul's words I. Cor. 12, 6: "There is a diversity of operations but the same God works in all."

## THE MEANING OF THE NAME YHWH AND THE LOGOS

In the beginning, there was only God and all that exists in the spiritual or material realm was born in a process of divine "unfolding." In that "Nothing" of which humans can know nothing, God is the inner impulse, unfolding at the ten sefirot levels; the latter are creative *logoi,* divine creative words.[11] They are the names of God, imbued with divine wisdom, active forces.[12] In his beautiful introduction to the Sefirot tree at the beginning of his lectures on Matthew's Gospel, Rudolf Steiner called the teaching of the Sefirot "Jewish spiritual science."[13] Each stage unfolds from the preceding one, and carries over to the next stage its metamorphosed forces. The ten sefirot are not mediators between God and the human being, nor are they "excrescences" or subdivisions; they are fully divine elements, self-cohesive and transformative. *They are God, not God's creation* emanating from God's forces. The material world and the spiritual world, with their hierarchies, are contained within them....[14]

The divine name YHWH is the expression of this entire divine self-unfolding, from *Y* (which stands for the first and second sefirot ("Nothing" and the highest "Wisdom") to the *H* that represents the third sefira (the highest level of the Elohim-forces), the *W* standing for the fourth to ninth sefirot and signifying the deeper levels of the divine names Elohim, EL, and YHWH, as we encounter them in the Bible especially

10. Maimonides, op. cit, I ch. 64.
11. Gershom Scholem, *Die Geheimnisse der Schöpfung,* p. 31 ff.
12. Rudolf Steiner: GATB 727, *Taschenbücher Diaries,* p. 220.
13. Rudolf Steiner, GA 123, *The Gospel of St. Matthew,* p. 244 ff.
14. Gershom Scholem, *Ursprung und Anfänge der Kabbala,* p. 83; Diether Lauenstein, *Der Messias,* p. 232.

before Abraham. The final *H* signifies the tenth sefira. From the first to the tenth sefira, the divine process proceeds from the most occult to the most accessible to human experience.... The tenth and last sefira is called Malkut, Kingdom.... It is the boundary, the transition from God to creature.... It represents the Logos, and Jewish mystics call it the Divine "I."[15] This last sefira ... is "near" to the earthly world and in particular to the human being; it is the link with the whole history of God, his people Israel, and Moses.

The Logos is the divine principle of the "I" or I AM. In the "I," the human being experiences the greatest proximity to God.[16]

Thus we can say that YHWH, the divine name, expresses the following:

1. The self-unfolding of the Divine outside of creation

2. The creative cosmic Word (Logos)

3. The "inner being" of God within the celestial and terrestrial worlds created by the Logos. This "inner being" expresses itself in God's benevolent aspect when YHWH is mentioned in the Bible (Exodus 34:7).

## The Approach to the Logos to Human Beings

If we read the Bible and Apocrypha carefully, we are struck by the fact that in many cases the word YHWH does not stand alone, but is connected with the term *Ka'vod*, which can be translated as splendor, honor, or glory. The Bible, as well as rabbinic and kabbalistic texts, refers to *Ka'vod* or *Shekinah* (meaning "God's dwelling") as the divine principle that appeared to the Israelites in the desert and to Moses upon Mount Sinai, that spoke out of the luminous cloud and the pillars of fire, and that later took the form of two cherubim on the Ark of the Covenant. Generally

---

15. Gershom Scholem, *Die jüdische Mystik in ihrer Hauptströmungen*, p. 236.

16. The relationship between Malkut and the human "I" has been expounded by Rudolf Steiner, GA 123, op. cit., p. 147 ff.

speaking, the names Shekinah and Ka'vod do not designate the tenth sefira (Logos) directly, but rather a divine light emanating from it, in which the forces of the tenth sefira are contained at a lower level of sanctity, reminiscent of John's verse (John:14): "and the Word became flesh and lived among us and we saw his glory."[17] In its purely divine form, the Logos could not be in direct contact with the human being. This is why the incarnation of the Christ Logos was produced indirectly by the intervention of the Christ archangel. Moses wanted to contemplate God's glory (Ka'vod) directly in the pure form of the tenth sefira, but God answered: "No person can see me and remain alive" (Ex. 33:18ff).[18]

## The Messiah-Light as the Sublime Solar Spirit

According to what was said above, *Kav'od* or the *Shekinah* may designate God in his pure, uncreated Logos aspect or designate an uncreated and invisible spiritual light inherent in the Logos in an attenuated form, also called the Holy Spirit. Its lower form is Sophia; its higher form is the second sefira Chokma (or heart of the inferior world). This light has no form but it has a voice.[19] As Gershom Scholem puts it here, *Kav'od* and *Shekinah* can have such a double meaning because "they are situated at the border between the created and the uncreated, and shine forth on both sides of that boundary."

Besides the "light" Logos (internal, invisible, unformed), Jewish esoterism also knows a second type of *Kav'od*. It can take the most diverse appearances and is also called "the body of the *Shekinah*" (*Gufha Schechina* or *Schiur Koma*). It is the cherubim in Ezekiel's vision. Cherubim are characteristically able to assume a diversity of forms: as angels, animals, or human

---

17. Hanspeter Ernst, *Die Schekhina in rabbinischen Gleichnissen*, p. 61.
18. Also Maimonides, ibid.
19. Gershom Scholem, *Ursprung ...*, p. 85; *Die jüdische Mystik ...*, pp. 120–121.

beings. The cherubim riding a divine chariot has human form. It is sometimes called the Angel of Creation because it contains the creative forces of the Logos in its inner self, in the form of the invisible, shapeless *Ka'vod*.[20]

We can suggest here that the spiritual body of the Shekinah, in which the Logos is immanent, is a solar spirit, Rudolf Steiner's Christ, the light body of the Logos whose form is also contemplated in the mysteries. Jewish sources also mention a messianic event concealed behind the manifestations of *Ka'vod* or *Shekinah*.

In Isaiah 60:1, it says: "Arise, shine! For thy light is come and the glory of the Lord is risen upon thee." This light, appearing at the same time as the glory of God (*Ka'vod*) is regularly identified with the Messiah. In an old rabbinic commentary on this passage of Isaiah (Isaiah 60:1-2),[21] there is a reference to Psalm 36:10 regarding this light: "For with thee is the fountain of life, and by thy light we shall see light." The commentary explains that when Israel peered into the horizon, this light was the Messiah-Light, coming from the primeval spiritual light of the first day of creation (Genesis 1:4). It was born before the creation of the universe and of the human being. Note that the Messiah-Light is contained within another light, as the Christ-Logos is sheathed in the sublime solar spirit. In the Midrash, quoted above, it is also said that God designated four "living beings" who will bear the chariot of the Messiah's glory, a clear reference to Ezekiel's vision.[22] We also find in the Talmud another confirmation of the identity between the Jewish Messiah-Light and Christ the sublime solar spirit. There, Psalm 72.17 is used as proof that the name of the Messiah predates creation: "Eternal is his name risen before the sun." We find similar identifications between *Shekinah* or *Ka'vod* and Christ in the Christian sources, for

---

20. Gershom Scholem, *Ursprung…* p.186, ff. on the relation between the Logos and the cherubim; see also Scholem, *Die jüdische Mystik.* p. 123. Scholem assumes that the cherubim was none other than a metamorphosis of the Logos.

21. *Midrash,* Pesikta Rabbati 36; see Günter Stemberger, *Midrasch,* p.170.

22. Stemberger, ibid.

instance, in Pietist literature.[23] In I Cor. 10.1-4, it is said that
the Israelites were baptized by the clouds and had drunk from a
spiritual rock that followed them, which was the Christ. As we
know, YHWH-*Ka'vod* proclaimed God's glory from the luminous cloud.[24]

## THE COSMIC MESSIAH IN JUDAISM

Anthroposophy allowed us to discover the cosmic Christ in
Judaism. As we saw above, the Logos plays a central role in
the Jewish conception of the divine. Like the Logos (which
for anthroposophy is the essence of the cosmic Christ Event),
the tenth sefira is active behind all worldly events. The second entity in the cosmic aspect of the Christ impulse, the
sublime Sun-Spirit Christ, can be found in the Messiah-Light
and in the visible *Ka'vod* of Ezekiel's vision of the divine chariot. In the many kabbalistic writings where cherubim are
mentioned, we find imaginations reminiscent of the Christ
archangel. Judaism also has a Messiah that is related to a
higher level of the cosmos, the prototype of the higher levels
of the evolution of the soul: *Neshamah, Kayah,* and *Yekidah.*[25]
These can be placed parallel with the Spirit Self, the Life
Spirit, and the Spirit Man.

## THE APPEARANCE OF THE ROYAL MESSIAH IN THE FUTURE
## AND THE FUTURE DESTINY OF THE JEWISH PEOPLE

In Judaism, as in anthroposophy, the advent of redemption is
a complex process occurring on several levels simultaneously
over a long period of time, and involving more than one spiritual entity. Hebrew sources mention a royal Messiah, whose
appearance will end all wars, specifically the war of Gog and

---

23. Cf. Mathias Morgenstern, in "Contributions à la compréhension du
Judaïsme," in *Judaica*, March 2000, volume I, p. 256.
24. Also Luke 21, 27; Daniel 7, 13.
25. Cf. Gershom Scholem, *Von der mystischen Gestalt der Göttheit*, p. 236.

Magog against the Jewish people. When it returns from exile, the Jewish people will be reinstalled in its homeland and all peoples will go on a yearly pilgrimage to Zion (Jerusalem) to receive divine teaching and attend the Feast of the Tabernacle (Micah 4 ff.; Zechariah 12ff; 14:16). The reign of the royal Messiah takes place in historical time, but is of short duration, and is preliminary to true redemption, at which point there will be a resurrection in a future world (*Haolam haba*), suggesting that the two events (the preliminary reign and the decisive deliverance) take place simultaneously in parallel worlds.[26]

The singularity of the incarnation of the Logos in the archangel Christ 2000 years ago does not mean that things had come to an end, and that is also the anthroposophical point of view: there is a gradual process demanding the active participation of human beings. The Mystery of Golgotha was excluded from the external faith of Judaism, thus allowing the Gentiles access to messianic salvation, (that is, the Christ impulse that the people of Israel has been serving ever since its origin). Israel must step back and is not allowed to contemplate the advent of Golgotha "until the fullness of all nations have found salvation" (Rom.11:25). During this time, the mystery of post-Christic Judaism remains hidden from Christianity. Paul was certain that there would be a new appearance of the Messiah and that it would involve the Jewish people, and he says, "And thus all of Israel will be saved, for it has been written: "the Redeemer will come out of Zion" (Rom. 11:26-28) ... "for the gifts and the calling of God are irrevocable ..." (Rom. 11:29).

Paul had nothing more precise to say about this future appearance of the Savior out of Zion. For Rudolf Steiner, this appearance concerns and depends upon the etheric realm, and will only be perceived in the future course of evolution. He felt

---

26. Daniel Krochmalnik, *Die Zweidimensionale Eschatologie des Maimonides*, in *Judaica*, June 1996, 2.121; Moritz Zobel, *Gottes Gesalbter. Der Messias und die messianische Zeit*, in *Talmud & Midrash*, 21 ff.

certain that the Jews had a future mission regarding the Christ.[27] He officially defended Judaism against anti-Semitic attacks on Jews' "attachment to outdated religious rituals and their keeping apart from other people."[28] It thus seems unfounded to say that Rudolf Steiner considered that the Jewish people should have dissolved after the advent of Christ, an erroneous interpretation by anthroposophists with a very limited knowledge of his life and work, on the basis of misunderstood oral statements on his part. This interpretation would have contradicted what Paul says (Steiner's source), as well as other things he himself said and did.

> Ben Zoma said:
>
> Who is wise? One who learns from all:
> "From all my teachers I gained insight."
> (Psalm 119:99)
>
> Who is strong? One who controls the self:
> "Better to have self control than to conquer a city." (Proverbs 16:32)
>
> Who is rich? One who desires only what is given: "When you eat the fruit of your labors, be happy and it shall be well with you." (Psalm 128:2)
>
> IV:1
>
> (From the Pirke Avot)

---

27. Ludwig Tieben, *Das Rätsel des Judentums* p. 254/256.
28. Rudolf Steiner, GA 31, *Gesammelte Aufsätze zur Kultur und Zeitgeschichte 1887-1901*, p. 378, 394 ff., 397, 409.

# 8

## THE INDIVIDUAL AND THE UNITY OF HUMANKIND
### AN ACCOUNT OF THE ZIONIST AND ANTHROPOSOPHIST ERNST MÜLLER

### BY HANS JÜRGEN BRACKER

*from* NOVALIS *May 1977*
*translated with supplementary annotations by Mado Spiegler*

### THE SIGNIFICANCE OF THE CHRIST PHENOMENON

Anthroposophy describes an anthropology of the permanent evolution of consciousness: increasing freedom, but also growing responsibility for one's own destiny, the destiny of other human beings, and the destiny of the earth and world. The goal of cosmological anthropology: free human beings as collaborators of divine creation through repeated incarnations. In the complex unfolding of world evolution, the story of Christ and Golgotha constitutes a central articulation, the expression of impulses and forces aiming at the freedom of all human beings and the realization of their eternal individuality.... The incarnation of Christ in a human body and his death at Golgotha marked a turning point in the whole of human evolution, and with the Mystery of Golgotha, the history of the human "I" really began.

Individuals are embedded in a family, a tribe, a nation, a religion that, from the standpoint of reincarnation, are fluid and transitory realities. In each incarnation, in a particular national group, the human being experiences another facet of universal human reality, a particular color of the spectrum of human-kind. Anthroposophy has been particularly sensitive—although not alone in this sensitivity—to the tension between evolution toward individuality and spiritual freedom on the one hand, and on the other, the increasingly illusionary and oppressive forces of nationalism since the end of the nineteenth century, holding back humanity from its timely development.[1]

## RUDOLF STEINER ON THE SUBJECT OF ZIONISM AND ANTI-SEMITISM

Steiner's opinions on many subjects, including Christianity and, in this case, Zionism and anti-Semitism, are not always easy to fully grasp—not only because, as Steiner himself unceasingly pointed out, his ideas were constantly evolving, but also because he would develop them from occasion to occasion in response to specific questions and always in the context of encounters with particular human beings. Only a few of these occasions are recorded, for scholars are only now beginning to dig through the vast amounts of material in the Steiner archives.

The need to overcome nationalism was one of the central themes of his social agenda. It is no surprise, then, that like other intellectuals of his time, including many distinguished Jewish intellectuals, he looked askance at Zionism, calling it "the enemy of Judaism." This opinion was expressed in an article on the First Zionist Congress held in Basel in 1897. Anti-Semitism he considered "not a serious problem at this point," "a childish foolishness," while conceding that things might change, and noting that attitudes toward the emigration to Palestine had changed considerably over a period of ten years and might well change even more in the future.

---

1. Cf. Grillparzer's famous formula: "From humanity through nationality to bestiality."

Four years later (1901) he was collaborating with the Newsletter of the Movement of Defense against Anti-Semitism, whose
founder and editor was his friend Ludwig Jacobowski.[2] In that
article, he indicated that "anti-Semitism endangers all of us, not
just the Jews.... It proceeds from an irrational mentality
... encourages unhealthy thinking ... and anyone with a philosophical turn of mind has to see it as a disquieting phenomenon...." During the intervening years, the Dreyfus Affair
had erupted in France, unleashing virulent waves of anti-Semitism, while Eastern Europe was the scene of pogroms.

In 1917, Steiner wrote two memoranda on the problem of
nationalities, attacking President Wilson's plans for a restruc-
turing of the international environment around the concept of
national self-determination narrowly understood as the right
for each people to have its own state.[3] As Steiner perceived it,
the myth of the culturally homogeneous nation-state, far from
ensuring peace as Wilson hoped, would instead make the twentieth century one of "unending wars and infinite human suffering," further compounded if the nation-states were "theocratic
states" based on religion at a point in history where evolution
demands the separation of church and state, the unconditional
recognition of religious and intellectual freedom as the private
privilege of emancipated citizens.

The threefold social organism, as Steiner conceived it, was
based on anti-nationalist premises. In 1922 he again expressed
his rejection of a Jewish state in Palestine, if it were to mean
that a non-Jew could not be accepted there as a full-fledged citizen. But when Ernst Müller got involved in translating the

---

2. *Verschämter Antisemitismus* in *Mitteilungsblatt aus d. Verein zur Abwehr des Antisemitismus* (reproduced in GA 31).
3. This meant the destruction of the multi-national state, and the political
recognition of long-struggling national identities. However, it also meant in a
number of cases the criminalization of small minority languages and culture
through the imposition of fictitious cultural unity upon groups that were historically related but had distinct languages.

*Threefold Social Organism* into modern Hebrew, Steiner agreed that a "multicultural" Palestine might indeed be a good testing ground for his ideas. In 1922, however, at the same time that he was denouncing the dangers of the populist movement in Europe, his 1897 statement was reprinted—arguably, without his permission, but also without his opposition—much to Ernst Müller's dismayed puzzlement, expressed in a letter in which he reminded Steiner of statements he had made to Müller in private conversations.

## JUDAISM AND ESOTERIC CHRISTIANITY:
## VIENNA AND PALESTINE

One way to summarize Ernst Müller's anthroposophic career is as an enterprise to enrich Christianity through the study of esoteric Judaism, and to enrich Judaism through the study of esoteric Christianity.

Moravian-born Ernst Müller (1880-1954) was a Zionist from his youth. In 1907, after military service and studies in Vienna, he emigrated to Palestine, one of the very first Western European Jews to do so, where he taught in Jaffa for two years. By then, the question of the place of Christianity in his personal life and in the life of the Jewish community had already been on his mind for about ten years. Soon after his return to Europe two years later, he encountered Rudolf Steiner at his Prague lectures, which he attended with his Theosophist brother Edmund (who would be deported out of the ghetto of Minsk in 1941). In later years he described those years as a time of profound transformation, of deepening involvement with Jewish esoteric religion, with Zionism, and with Christianity, and as the beginning of his activity as a writer, editor, translator, and teacher.

He was attracted by Achad Chaam and Martin Buber's idea of building in Palestine and Jerusalem a center for the renewal of Judaism, to liberate the Jews from the psychological scar-tissue of oppression and to open the way from old, rigid religious forms to the free religion of the future. Zionism for him was "a path from the inner ghetto to a liberated humanity, albeit in the form of the modern nation." By recapitulating in its own ranks the experience of European national development, Zionism might be the structure through which the cosmic Christ could be accessed.

### FREE RELIGION AND ANTHROPOSOPHY: A CONTROVERSIAL BRIDGE-BUILDER

At the foundation of anthroposophy was the idea of Christ as cosmic event, an evolutionary development of humanity, to be expressed in the birth of a free Christianity. Although this eventually gave birth to the Christian Community, it had not been Steiner's intention to create a new religion. Regarding Judaism, if the Jews' special mission in the evolution of humanity was considered to have ended with the birth of Christ, Steiner had also made various statements (to which Robert Lissau and Ernst Müller had been privy) about the ongoing "streaming of Jehovah forces out of the East," the idea that "one day the Jews would again have a mission in relation to Christ," the anticipated role of Judaism as "spiritualizing a Christianity caught in the throes of a materialist spirituality." They took these statements with utmost seriousness: whatever the future might hold, there was no doubt in Müller's mind, or in that of the young Zionists who attended his anthroposophical study groups, that Judaism was the necessary vessel of personal and social transformation.

In 1911, Steiner had told Müller that "the most remarkable Jewish individuals are in the Zionist movement,"[4] and Müller himself felt a great opening toward anthroposophy and Waldorf education among those very Eastern Jews nurtured by esoteric Judaism. In fact, anthroposophy attracted both very assimilated

---

4. Quoted by Müller in his autobiographical *Geistige Spuren in Lebenserinnerungen.*

German or Austrian Jews and Eastern Jews, although there were unmistakable class tensions between the two groups.[5] Müller was by then teaching at the Hebrew Teacher's College in Vienna, writing many articles on the Kabbalah, Jewish linguistics, and the Psalms, as well as articles on mathematical subjects and other aspects of anthroposophy, and authoring the first German translation of the Zohar[6] with both Steiner's and Buber's encouragement. He was also conducting extremely well-attended anthroposophic study groups, with about sixty long-term students, many of whom came from the Zionist youth movement, and among them a number of later pillars of the Anthroposophical Society. [7]

As a member of the mathematical-astronomical section of the society he had warm relations with Elizabeth Vreede and George Kaufmann (Adams), whose help was decisive when he emigrated to England in the late 1920s.

Many individuals came to anthroposophy out of Judaism and played an important role in the movement.[8] After 1933, spurred by uncertainty about the eventual fate of Switzerland in a national-socialist Europe, a number of them, including

---

5. The year 1922 presented Müller with several crises; one of them was the organization—with a great deal of publicity—of the West-East Congress. Publicity was deliberately downplayed in neighborhoods inhabited by Eastern European Jewish immigrants; this was attributed to the fact that they were considered rabble by the more "bourgeois" members. Müller expressed his dismay at this avoidance, on petty grounds, of individuals who had a lot to offer spiritually.

6. This translation is considered a "classic" and has been reprinted repeatedly over the years.

7. Such as, Maria and Hella Spira; Otto Fränkl; Norbert Glas and his wife-to-be Maria Deutsch; Egon Lustgarten and Hugo Kauder; and Erwin Piskati, later Philipps.

8. For instance, as early as 1903-04 Adolf Arenson and Carl Unger; after 1918, Karl Koenig and his collaborators in the foundation of the Camphill movement; Walter Johannes Stein; Maria Roschl-Lehrs, leader of the youth section; Alexander Strakosch; George Kaufman (Adams); the painters Richard and Hilde Pollak; the composer Viktor Ullmann.

Müller and friends, moved to England—with a resultant
upswing in anthroposophic activity there. Others went to the
United States, a few to Palestine. Müller's students were the
originators of a range of anthroposophic ventures in Israel.[9]
Many others did not manage to emigrate. There are only two
published accounts by concentration camp survivors.[10]

### ERNST MÜLLER ON THE FUTURE OF JUDAISM
### AND THE UNITY OF HUMANKIND

For many Jews who had been attracted to one or another
prospect of an overarching human culture transcending old
religious divisions, World War II was a harsh setback. As far as
Ernst Müller was concerned, the events had, if anything, confirmed the need to work in depth toward the unity of humankind. He wrote in 1945 in an unpublished manuscript:

Today as in the past, Judaism is marked by its emphasis on
this concept of the unity of mankind. While it is often a
mere philosophical abstraction for others … it is for Jews
an existential reality, the very life-substance of their identity. Unity of the Heart, unity of Mankind, unity of God
are wonderfully expressed in the Psalmist's prayer "Let my
heart be undivided in reverence for your name" (Ps.
86,11). Certainly Jewish intellectuals have their share of
responsibility for the disintegration of this aspiration:
experimental psychology, psychoanalysis, aestheticism are
the fragmented remnants of this concept of human unity.

---

9. These include Waldorf schools, curative communities, biodynamic agricul-
ture, and an anthroposophic kibbutz.
Cf. Uri ben-David, *Der aktuelle Stand der anthroposophischen Tätigkeit in Israel*, in *Novalis*, 2/3,1994.
10. Martha Haarburger, *Erinnerungen aus dem Konzentrationslager Theresienstadt* in
*Die Christengemeinschaft*, 5/1978, and Lotte Beran, *Ein Jahr Konzentrationslager Auschwitz* in *Christengemeinschaft*, 7/1978.

The most important reality is the unity of mankind. All of biblical history is founded upon it, in the connection between the Old and New Testaments. And if the idea of a chosen people seems to contradict this unity, then this idea must be purified of any hint of arrogance. It is the great task of the Jewish people both to stop considering themselves an exceptional people and at the same time to accept that fate and put it in the service of human unity. I shall evoke an image, and again this must be devoid of any kind of arrogance: it is Judah Halevi's image of the heart being at the same time the weakest organ of the body and the center of the human organism.

The third unity is the unity of God. Clearly, in order to awaken for itself and for the world the inmost sources of life, Judaism will have to overcome the narrow concept of God found in rabbinic thought, and accept the Christian idea of the God of Love, as indeed it is foreshadowed in the Zohar. The idea of the living trinity, cleansed of any dogmatism, is theologically fundamental. For Judaism, the task will consist in emphasizing the unity in the trinity, as against any tendencies to either favor or reject one or the other of the three principles. Only through a clear understanding of the unity in the multiplicity, and through the acknowledgment of the intimate connection between Old and New Testaments, will a point be reached in which future anti-Jewish tendencies in Christianity as well as anti-Christian tendencies in Judaism will be nipped in the bud.

The philosophy of Franz Rosenzweig, Martin Buber or, in our time, Emmanuel Levinas,[11] all represent steps in this direction.

---

11. See *Novalis*, 3/97.

## LONDON

In 1941, Ernst Müller and Frieda Schorr were married in the presence of old Viennese friends by Rabbi Moritz Bauer, Müller's childhood friend. An hour before the wedding, Müller had participated in the class meeting of the anthroposophical society. When he died in 1954, he was buried in the Jewish cemetery at Golders Green, and the memorial service was held at the Christian Community church in Hampstead, thus emphasizing the bridging quality of his life.

## EPILOGUE

When the Christian Community was founded in 1922, many anthroposophists saw in it the crowning of anthroposophy; whole sections joined *en masse*, a move that Rudolf Steiner viewed as a distressing sign of the misunderstanding of his intentions. He also took enthusiastic reports of long-time anthroposophists being formally baptized as evidence of misunderstanding. Ernst Müller himself was never baptized, but the article that he sent from his deathbed to be published in the Christian Community newsletter was about names, and his signature included a new name: Michael, a name that is both Jewish and Christian.

> The name is the precise point at which a human being or thing comes into the sphere of sound and tone. This is true even of God, the utterly unattainable: although we cannot see or talk to him directly, the act of uttering (or even writing the letters of) his name calls up his presence in the human being.[12]

---

12. Ernst-Michael Müller, "Names," in *Christian Community*, August, 1954.

# 9

# Between Martin Buber and Rudolf Steiner: Hugo Bergman in Martin Buber's Biography

## by Gerhard Wehr

*from* Das Goetheanum *January 1986*

*translated by Annette Conlon, edited by Fred Paddock*

Whenever we enquire about the spiritual pioneers of the late nineteenth century we encounter human contradictions and karmic inconsistencies. "Those who want to prepare the ground for friendliness could not be friendly themselves," Bertold Brecht once remarked. And those who set out to lay the foundation for an encompassing cultural renewal—leading representatives of anthroposophy included—were often lacking in a culture of human interaction. Of course, it is doubtless the special task of founding personalities to concentrate on the fulfillment of their mission. This demands the gathering of all forces, not necessarily leaving those personalities the ability to engage in an appropriate dialogue with contemporary spiritual streams. This shortcoming is even more surprising in human beings who spent their lives striving to build spiritual bridges. This makes it especially important to look at the Israeli philosopher Hugo Bergman (1878-1965) as he stands between Martin Buber and Rudolf Steiner.

Martin Buber's work is characterized by three major achievements: he is known as one of the leading representatives of dialogic thinking; he is a mediator as well as interpreter of Hasidic mysticism, a spiritual movement born in eighteenth-century Central Europe; and he is a noted translator into German of the Old Testament. From the point of view of today, Martin Buber is also highly relevant due to the fact that—long before Israel was founded; that is, in the early days of Zionism—Buber was committed to a binational state in Palestine, giving full equality to Palestinians and Jews, an idea that today seems more utopian than ever. Interestingly, having gone through a mystical phase early on, his later focus was almost exclusively on the principle of dialogue, with an almost total lack of interest in spiritual research, including the work of Rudolf Steiner.

Between the two men, with whom he had formed deep friendships, stood Hugo Bergman, in whom differing threads of destiny interwove, and who was seemingly predestined to bring forth a connection between Buber's dialogical philosophy and Steiner's spiritual science. Bergman's cultural and historical significance include being the first Western Jew in this century to write books of a Jewish and philosophical character in Hebrew; creating a Hebrew terminology for modern philosophical concepts; sponsoring a range of philosophical translations—Steiner's work included; founding the National Library in Palestine in 1920; participating soon thereafter in the creation of Brit Shalom, the first organization for peace between Jews and Arabs; teaching at Hebrew University, where he regularly taught a course on the *Philosophy of Freedom*; and his personal role as friend to a wide range of students and visitors, who always found him an open listener.

His diaries and letters (published in 1984) tell how the young philosopher, a student of Franz Brentano, found his way to Rudolf Steiner's Prague lectures in the home of Berta Fanta, the local leader of the Theosophical Society and later Bergman's mother-in-law. It was in Prague also, and just a short time later, that Bergman attended Martin Buber's influential talks on Judaism in the Prague circle of Bar-Kochba. Thereafter, Bergman's life as a philosopher and human being unfolded between the work of these two personalities.

Buber's philosophy, as we know, is impelled by the leitmotiv of the relationship of "I and Thou," and further, the tension between the earthly "I" and the eternal "Thou" of God. With this, the question of cognition is relativized.... In a conversation with scientists and philosophers of his time, Buber described his position as follows: "If I strive to explain the fact of man, I can never leave out of sight that 'Man lives before God', but at no point can I include God Himself in my explanation, just as little as I can detach God's undoubted working in history from the history, in order to make God an object of my research."[1] Or elsewhere, we have Buber's skeptical question "What is it to us if there are higher worlds?"[2]

As much as Bergman in principle agreed with Buber's philosophy of dialogue, he saw Buber's comments as a drastic oversimplification. Despite his acknowledgment of the indispensable categories of "Person" and "Other," Bergman felt he had to reject Buber's renunciation of gnosis. He does so thus: "Toward the higher worlds, we have the duty of cognizing, just as much as we have the duty of cognizing the world of the senses. I cannot explain Buber's rejection of this responsibility of cognizing higher worlds, other than that Buber, repelled by the aberrations of Gnostic activities in times of decadence, wanted to set up a barrier against an unhealthy curiosity that can only lead to disaster, as the Gnostics themselves constantly emphasized.... Nevertheless, it seemed to me that Buber's thinking here is caught in a rationalistic prejudice, held hostage to the worldviews of the nineteenth century...." Bergman adds that "... it is very important to break through these barriers nowadays, if one wants to carry Buber's own

---

1. Paul Schilpp and M. Friedman, *Martin Buber,* in the series "Library of Living Philosophers," p. 690.
2. In *Die Chassidische Botschaft,* p. 156.

thoughts further toward that "larger reality" of which (his) early work bears witness and towards which his whole life work points."[3]

As to the outcome of the two friends' spiritual struggle, Bergman recounts Buber's answer to his question about the legitimacy of Rudolf Steiner's spiritual research. "He said he was not against someone doing research in that area, only it was none of his (Buber's) business: there was plenty enough for him to explore in the immediate world at hand; to which I responded that the same argument could be used by others against (Buber) when they say they can't be bothered with such far-fetched stuff. He then told me of spiritualists who maintained that they had contacted spouses dead for ten years, and that about such things he could only remain silent."[4] Clearly Buber stood far removed from the concerns and approaches of anthroposophical spiritual science; and, according to Bergman's diary, they never really came to a mutual understanding. Buber once attended a lecture by Steiner and could not stand the atmosphere, while at the same time mentioning that he would no doubt have plenty of time in his next life to find out about these things.

Bergman's relationship with Rudolf Steiner had several facets. Steiner's work meant enough to him that he took it with him when he was called to the front during World War I, which he experienced from beginning to end as an officer in the Austrian army.... In a diary entry of January 1917 he mentioned, "The rereading of Steiner's books was very useful to me. The thoughts, the living concepts, the explanation of the organism in that context, the theory of evolution centered on consciousness rather than on some 'mechanical switch,' the discussions about Newton and Goethe's color theory and the limitations of natural-scientific concepts revealed by these

---

3. Op cit., Schilpp and Friedman, p. 308.
4. Conversation with Buber, October 30, 1957.

disputes, and the clear formulations of Steiner's *Riddles of Man* have been very helpful to me."

His perception of Steiner during the years of the Threefold movement were of Steiner as "a politician through and through."[5] In later years, there was a certain distancing from Steiner's work, although never from Steiner the person, which Bergman explained thus to a friend: "Just like you, perhaps, I have sought for help in anthroposophy, and for reasons similar to yours perhaps, I have turned away from it. However, I received much from the personal contact with Dr. Steiner, and also still read his lectures once in a while, and believe that there is much that is right in the development of the forces that anthroposophy talks about...." And again: "If we are going to speak of spiritual exercises or of getting close to God, we shouldn't talk of a kind of spiritual gymnastics. Instead, I see just one single exercise: to constantly educate ourselves to experience the world as a neverending message (*Botschaft*) to us. Again and again, when we sink into the bustling business of the day, or when, as now (1940) the waves of despair threaten to engulf us, spiritual exercises consist in trying once again to pronounce the blessing 'on the One through whose Word all things have become'. When Steiner asks, 'how do we attain the knowledge of higher worlds?' a question which has preoccupied me throughout the years, this is the answer that comes to mind, one which Buber has brought particularly close to me...."

Later comments by Bergman make clear that this did not mark a renunciation of Steiner, but rather the beginning of a process of clarification. According to his own account, Bergman never became an anthroposophist. The septuagenarian once commented with a certain resignation, "It is a fact that I

5. H. Bergman, *Tagebücher und Briefe 1901-1975*, 1988 (entry of 1919). This is an interesting remark in view of the fact that, in later years, Bergman himself and his followers often regretted that his influence in the actual politics of Israel was limited by his being, in the end, more philosopher than politician.

did not manage the whole Steiner complex and all that goes with it. I had become too much of a mystic to stay a philosopher, and too little of a 'mystic' to cross over completely. So I stayed in-between...."[6]

This staying in-between should not be interpreted as simple indecisiveness, neither in Hugo Bergman nor in many others. In Bergman's case, it was this position of positive critical attitude toward anthroposophy and its founder that enabled him to achieve manifold mediations and to act as a bridge builder. For more than six decades, Bergman thus assumed the special task that destiny had assigned him. Results were sometimes slim: an attempt to bring about a meeting between Einstein and Steiner merely resulted in convincing the physicist to attend a lecture by Steiner. But, as mentioned above, in his position as professor and writer, his own personal qualities as a man of dialogue greatly contributed to the work of anthroposophy in Israel, despite the controversies to which he was exposed, sharing in this the general fate of bridge builders, as if the knowledge of a reality could be comprehended exclusively from the ideological compound on this side of the bridge or on the other side. In a world where bridge builders are more important than ever, Bergman's memory deserves to be honored.

Hillel used to say:
If I am not for myself, who will be for me?
If I am only for myself, what am I?
And if not now, when?

I:14
(from the *Pirke Avot*)

---

6. From *Tagebücher und Briefe.*, op. cit.

# 10

# CHOSEN DESTINY

BY RUDI LISSAU

*from* THE GOLDEN BLADE 48, *The Image of Blood*

THE PROVOCATIVE SITUATION in which I was once asked how an anthroposophist could incarnate as a Jew prompted me to answer: "One of the advantages might be to have been spared the ministrations of the traditional churches."

I am intensely aware of the fact that I, born in 1911, was able to incarnate in a family deeply devoted to Rudolf Steiner. Never was there a time in my life in which I was not conscious of the existence of this unique man. My father and his brother—the latter to become the first secretary of the Goetheanum in the first years of the creation of this building—were among the eight people who early in the century founded the Theosophical Society in Vienna in order to provide a platform for Rudolf Steiner's activity in Austria.

Both my father and my mother were Jews, but father had already moved away from Judaism, while mother, when she married, was a liberal agnostic. It was a time when the problem of race had acquired a real fascination for "modern" people— today we might rather argue in terms of differing cultures or of sociological groups—and father had come under the influence of Otto Weininger, a brilliant young Jew who was filled by a hatred of women and a hatred of Jews. Father was also misled by Steiner's great respect for German culture, not seeing that this respect applied to the age of Goethe, Novalis, and the German idealistic philosophers, and unaware that Steiner had no truck with the nationalism and imperialism of Wilhelminian Germany.

But, typically for a Jew, however great his distance from Jewish life and Jewish religion became, he took no outward step towards separation from his ancestral religion in order not to hurt his parents. Only after their deaths could we openly and joyously celebrate Christmas. Until then we were simply spectators at the celebration of the Christian members of our household.

So my experience of Jewish religion was fairly remote. Once or twice a year I was sent to the synagogue, a rather embarrassing experience, while the religion lessons in school were simply a bore. But I enjoyed the occasional invitations to the Passover meal in the house of a rabbi, a personal friend of my father's. Such a meal is a family affair to which a few guests are invited and as the youngest member at the table I enjoyed a particular position. The meal is permeated by a truly human mood. Its ambience is not easy to describe for me as it is composed of different, indeed almost contradictory elements. A ritual, centuries old, and spontaneous light conversation and gentle humour and laughter, reminiscences and introspection, human warmth and devotion to God, the memory of past sufferings, the gratitude for having been spared during the last year. Paramount the undying hope: 'This year here, next year in Jerusalem."

As an adolescent I had taken a position not much different from that of many liberal Austrian Jews. I was not interested in Jewish religion and Jewish life. I was an Austrian, though occasionally handicapped by my Jewish ancestry. I shared the general dislike of Eastern European Jews in their distinct and alien attire who, unsettled by the First World War and its aftermath, came to Austria in large numbers. These were the people, I believed, who caused anti-Semitism. In other words, I had adopted a typically xenophobic attitude. We, of course, are all

right, but these people, whoever they might be, are inferior to
us. Their habits, their morals, their outward behavior make
them deeply suspect. I did not want to have anything to do
with them. Life was to teach me different.

In my early twenties I became a teacher of blind children and
for five years worked and lived among blind people. The insti-
tute which became my home was a relic of the Austro-
Hungarian Empire. Our pupils came from thirteen different
countries, particularly from Eastern Europe, many from Jewish
homes. They showed me how distorted my preconceptions of
Eastern European Jews were. Instead of a type, I came in touch
with individuals who showed as much variety of behavior and
appearance as "we Austrians."

My blind pupils, many of them to become victims of the
Holocaust, gave me an invaluable present: they freed me from
my feeling of inferiority as a Jew. From now on my Jewish
heredity was as much a karmic fact as my sanguine tempera-
ment, it had advantages and disadvantages, and was nothing to
be embarrassed about. More important, they conveyed to me
that the mood I had encountered at the Passover meals was not
a once-in-a-blue-moon phenomenon, but the climax of a basic
attitude which permeated every aspect of life throughout the
cycle of the year.

Throughout the fifties I was friends with a charming man, a
Catholic Rhinelander by birth, but an anthroposophist and
music teacher at the Basel Steiner school. A truly religious man,
he had left the Roman Church. Neither the Christian Community met his needs nor the esoteric School. But he felt a close
kinship to the religious meditations of Eastern European Jews.
His library contained many books of stories of Hasidic rabbis,
their deliberations and meditations. They opened a new world
to me: traditional Jewish piety nurtured a contemporary German in a way which neither traditional Christianity nor Rudolf
Steiner, whom he deeply appreciated, could give him. The
intense love of God of these rabbis and their disciplined

endeavour to fathom His mind in their meditations opened up to me a new dimension of Jewish life. Where else in Europe were there lay people—a rabbi is not a priest—with such a concern with questions of justice, of piety, of morality, of the good life? Where were other large groups of people for whom God mattered to this extent?

A third experience came in the seventies and eighties. In my work at the Wynstones Kindergarten Training Course I encountered a number of most interesting students from Israel. In their intellectual and religious dilemma concerning the central position of the new Christianity in Steiner's work they naturally turned to me hoping I could empathize with their predicament.

Through them I realized that their existential position was utterly different from that of former generations of Central and Eastern European Jews. They had a state, they were a nation, they had to come to terms with the reality of power. The inner glory and the outer tragedy of European Jewry had been and possibly still is their utter insecurity. They exemplified two general human truths: I live by the ministrations of those around me; and, the human Ego grows out of our own inner resources and out of our inner relation to God in His world of the spirit.

One of the difficulties when looking at a religion other than our own is that we presume they all hold practically the same beliefs, share a common form of life, and are utterly different from other confessional communities. So we fasten a particular label on a group of people, a dangerous attitude as I had found out in my prejudice concerning Eastern European Jews. What have "born-again Christians" of the southern States in common with Irish Catholics? What unites Zen Buddhists and Burmese generals, Tibetan lamas and followers of the "Living Buddha" in Japan? After the death of the founder, religious movements tend to split and splinter. Buddha gave us the Eightfold Path. Steiner recreated it in a modern, western way. Compare his version in *How to Know Higher Worlds*[1] with the formulation of modern Zen. The result may be utter bewilderment.

On the other hand, many religions arrive at an orthodoxy with clearly formulated tenets and contain, at the same time, forms of mysticism, ecstatic movements, and other forms of religious life not too dissimilar from those of other religions. One of my former pupils married a Bengali Hindu. The first-born was a son. Granny in Calcutta felt she had to fly to England to make sure that an equivalent to our baptism was celebrated, and celebrated in the most appropriate manner. The English grandfather, a religious man and an anthroposophist, asked to be present at the ceremony. He was anxious to experience the full depth of a religious act that arose in pre-Christian times, the living manifestation of an utterly different, more spiritual consciousness. He was bitterly disappointed. No religious experience, no emotional depth, simply a traditional ritual carried out to the letter. But this is exactly the attitude for which the Orthodox Jew is blamed. As long as everything is properly carried out, the success of a religious rite is assured. The participants need not experience great emotional depths, the celebrant need not be a person of outstanding morality. The Roman as well as the Orthodox churches look at the Eucharist as an *opus operatum*, a deed completed long ago, and independent of the morality of the celebrant.

Each religion is lived in a wide variety of life styles and—as my own experience as an adolescent taught me—it is only too easy to typecast one particular form of behavior as characteristic for the whole group. How often have I heard in Austria "if only all Jews were like you" or "like your family," particularly from people who had hardly ever met another Jew. One learned to accept such a statement and hoped that life would teach the person concerned to rise above his or her preconceptions. As

---

1. Anthroposophic Press, 1994.

long as we do not wean ourselves from typecasting the alien as Shylocks or Fagins, how can we be numbered among the followers of Christ as Steiner presented him: He came to all mankind, but to each one individually. To speak of Christian nations is a misunderstanding.

This situation is complicated by the belief that the Jews are the chosen people whom God bound to Himself in a sacred covenant. Through the way they lead their lives, through their suffering, they testify to the relevance of this covenant. This gives the religious Jew a feeling of superiority, sometimes even of arrogance. Like the Cathars of the Languedoc they are not surprised that the "world" is evil. Their conviction makes them look at the "world" as something rather inferior, and the covenant depends on maintaining a purity of blood.

This special and unique relationship to God results in a religious intensity unknown to most modern Christians. Every act of daily life is a sacred act. The householder wakes up and immediately walks to the window. He looks outside. Does nature look the same or has overnight the Messiah come? No food is taken without a grace being said, and there are a vast number of graces. There is one, say, for eating oranges, and a special grace for eating the first orange of the season.

The occult day, as Steiner confirms, begins at nightfall on the previous evening. For the Jew, then, the climax of the week is Friday evening, the eve of the Sabbath. I have not forgotten what Hannah told me. Among my blind pupils she was the gentlest as well as the most gifted, almost certainly a victim of the Holocaust. Her family was pitifully poor and hunger was not uncommon. But every Friday night there was the meal, celebrated in peace and joy, and amidst thanks to God for the food the family were able to eat in this, the first hour of the Sabbath. The small girl realized that the week's diet had to be kept to a minimum so that Friday could be celebrated in a dignified way.

When I see the Oberufer Three Kings Play I am very sensitive to the way in which the Jewish priests have been told to handle the Bible scrolls. Like the breviary of the priest in the Christian Community these scrolls are handwritten. In the synagogue three passages are read from the Bible and it is deemed a great honour if a person is chosen to read one of today's passages to the congregation. Whoever handles the scroll will do so with greatest care and the first act will be to kiss it. When the scroll becomes fragile with age it is not assigned to the waste paper basket, it is not even burned. God's word is given a proper funeral and is ritually buried. In present-day Israel, orthodox Jews speak Yiddish. How could you demean Hebrew, the language which God spoke, by using it when buying a bus ticket?

But it would be entirely erroneous to assume that Jewish piety and devotion exhausts itself in ritual practices, however appropriate and dignified. Although the intensity of the religious and spiritual life of the individual is not unique to Jewish life, the circumstances are unusual. For the spiritual activity takes place not in an *ashram* in a lonely Himalayan valley, but in a normal household which forms a protective mantle around the seeker for God, and its aim is only incidentally a mystic union. It has practical aims: how to solve a moral dilemma, how to advise a person in need, how to become a better person, how to increase God's kingdom on earth. In this specific sense Jewish life is unique. God's "command" to Abraham that his descendants should be a folk of priests finds its fulfilment in two ways: first, that the Jew is encouraged not to follow the commands of a priestly hierarchy, but to learn to act individually. Secondly, the realization that we are endowed for this work in different degrees and so we respect and support those who are best able to carry out this "command." So we see as one of the central realizations of Jewish culture the intense seeker of enlightenment who attempts to fathom some fragment of the mind of God and to appreciate its consequences for our moral and social life. Such a person is accompanied by a band of disciples, supported by a group of helpers, and respected by a much wider community. Jewish lore treasures the achievements of such individuals over long stretches of time. It is aware of knowledge that arose out of the total commitment of individuals, and understands that spiritual knowledge is personal and therefore multi-faceted.

Mention should be made here of two particular forms of Jewish religious life. First, the Hasidim, a movement (if I am not mistaken) only a couple of centuries old, the roots of which may well be buried in much older layers of Jewish culture. Hasidic Jews stress our emotional commitment to God which has priority over the strict ritual insisted on by the orthodox Jew. The man filled with the love of God is so full of joy that he will sing and dance. Much of Hasidic religious insight and experience speaks to us in the works of Martin Buber. People acquainted with Steiner are often strongly attracted by Buber's stories and absolutely amazed that "this man is not even a Christian, leave alone an anthroposophist."

The occult treasures of the Kabbalah are widely recognized. According to Professor Maurin, it antedates the book of Genesis and is the precious relic of the insights of people who still lived very close to the Divine World and its beings. Steiner knew that Kabbalah and in a number of places used images and concepts of this primeval lore. Today the teachings of the Kabbalah have fertilized much occult thinking, but in the first half of our century when Kabbalistic knowledge was still confined to a small circle, the greatest living scholar of the Kabbalah was Ernst Müller, one of the founders of the Vienna Theosophical Society. He emigrated to England where he was held in greatest esteem by George Adams who discussed occult as well as mathematical problems with him.

We shall now turn to Steiner. The picture of Yahweh which Blavatsky had given to theosophists was definitely negative: a harsh, judgmental, stern deity. But by 1911 Steiner had so far moved away from theosophical ideas that he was able, in Berlin on 13 March, to make the bold statement that Yahweh is *wesensgleich* with Christ. *"Wesensgleich"* is not a word generally used, but its most basic translation would be "identical." But it would seem best not to go for a hard-and-fast word at all. Just as the Divine Father and the Divine Son are aspects of the same divinity so Yahweh and Christ are manifestations of the same Being at different stages of approach to human perception.

What Yahweh revealed to Abraham and, at a later stage, to Moses forged together an often recalcitrant people who were to provide the body of the incarnate God, as well as, particularly in the work of the prophets, the concepts and images through which He could reveal Himself to earthly human beings.

Steiner is not so much interested in what Christ said, but in what He did. As I understand it, each statement of the Sermon on the Mount had already been said by one or an other Jewish prophet who preceded Christ by two or three centuries. Readers of Steiner's lecture on the Lord's Prayer may have felt disappointed that he did not dwell on the moral implications of these verses. But Steiner looks at the actual situation: Christ addresses a group of Jews. They know already in advance each statement in proportion to the degree in which they had opened themselves to the riches of their prophetic tradition. Steiner shows in this lecture how Christ selected those statements of this tradition which He could weave into a verbal texture revealing the fullness of the human being as a spiritual-physical totality.

Yahweh and Christ: the "One" chose Abraham and bade him assemble around him people, each one of them able to become a priest, to learn to take on individual responsibility and not to live the life of tribal masses subject to the will and whim of a superhuman king, the Son of Heaven. Jewish myth puts the position of Abraham, newly endowed with individual responsibility, into an impressive picture: he was the first man whose hair turned white. But the "Other" widened this challenge to embrace every human being, and died for all, that is for each human individuality. At first there was a relation from God to one chosen man who then conveyed this experience to the rest of the people chosen. But Christ works without a mediator. He approaches each one of us individually when He recognizes our potential to receive Him. Between these two distinct relationships stand, historically, the Jewish prophets. The last of them was John who witnessed the union of Christ and Jesus of Nazareth.

We can contemplate the close relationship of Jahve and Christ also by pondering the importance of the Meal. I mentioned the unique position, dignity and joy of the meal on Friday night. I recounted the impression which the Passover meal made on the little boy who had hardly any idea of what happened around him, but still was able to deeply appreciate the mood of this very special meal. And this was the meal which Christ hallowed and lifted up to establish the Eucharist and to lay the foundation, in word and deed, for the second half of the history of this planet, a process described by the orthodox churches as the Deification of Man.

Steiner welcomed the presence of Jews in Europe and hoped that the host nations would be liberal enough to open their societies to their Jewish fellow citizens so that the latter would gradually completely merge with their hosts. Conversely, he was perturbed by the beginning of Zionism. It reduced the importance of the Jews for the development of mankind. They had become a people spread over the whole globe and were in a position to accelerate the growing awareness of the spiritual unity of mankind, an essentially Christian impulse. Zionism however pointed them in the opposite direction, into nationhood and nationalism. The future was to show how justified his apprehension had been.

I now turn to specific remarks which Steiner made in Vienna. It was probably in the early twenties that he said he was unable to discuss two subjects there because he was painfully aware of the consequences of his words on the emotions of his audience: human sexuality and anti-semitism.

When an anthroposophist of long standing and a man with

a Jewish background asked: 'What is the task of the modern Jew?" Steiner answered thereby the question which this article posed at the beginning, and the answer is momentous: "His task is to spiritualize Christianity which the Catholic Church has ahrimanized and the Protestants intellectualized."

If we look at the quest of the modern Israeli, we see that the majority of Israelis are Sephardim, Jews who had lived in Muslim empires. So they are ignorant of traditional Christianity, but also mainly untouched by anti-Semitism because the Prophet had imbued his followers with respect for the "people of the Book." The emergence of the state of Israel—to a certain extent also the Balfour declaration—created terrible tension between Muslims and Jews, mainly in the political and not the religious field.

The European Jews who were the founding fathers of the state of Israel had been always in close proximity to Christianity. For them it had been impossible to remain indifferent. Some were filled with a secret longing for Christ, while others felt real hatred for Him. An outstanding example of the former group is Shalom Asch. This great Yiddish writer wrote a most interesting trilogy. *The Nazarene* describes the life of Christ according to the gospel of Judas which two men find early in the twentieth century. Judas had recognized the Christ, but realizing his divine power betrayed him in the expectation that He would now be forced to use his power and liberate the Jews from the Roman yoke. The second part of the trilogy is called *The Apostle* (that is, Paul), and the third part *The Mother* (the Virgin Mary).

But as far as I can probe, little is left in contemporary Israel either of the secret longing for Christ or of hatred. So it might seem that there is little left in contemporary Jewish awareness of a connection to Christ. This is particularly important as today definite efforts are under way at the Goetheanum to move the Anthroposophical Society from a Central European society into a multicultural one of global dimension.

This will be a formidable task and one for which we have little experience. But my work with young Israelis at the Wynstones Kindergarten Training Course makes me think that among them will be a sizeable number who will find Christ in a modern way, free from conventional shackles. Some will be stirred by contact with anthroposophical life. But the grace of Christ can awaken any human being, and in such a case it is only a question of finding the conceptual framework to explain the moment of recognition. There is only one other culture which before the Incarnation prepared the ground for an understanding of the Mystery of Golgotha in any way that approximates to the contribution of the Hebrew people. The ancient Greeks had given to the world the profound and intimate teaching of the Logos, the Divine Word which became the central conviction of the Gospel of St. John.

The Jewish tradition offers us the story of the Fall, the selection of Abraham, the mission of Moses, Solomon's temple, the prophetic tradition, John the Baptist and many of the statements which Christ made to His Jewish followers. They form a sound enough basis for any modern Jew who has been touched by the Christ impulse to recognize in his experience most of the features which were dear to him in his own culture. Such a person need only make the step from the blood-bound tribal religion of the "chosen people" to the world-wide humanitarian impulse which imbued many European Jews from the Age of Enlightenment right into our own time. Such a person will be helped by one of Steiner's central insights, the changing human consciousness, the process at the heart of history.

As I survey the destinies of people whom I have met personally, I conclude that a good part of anthroposophists who chose for their incarnation a Jewish background were filled with a deep longing for Christ, a longing which colored their whole stance within anthroposophy. An outstanding figure in this context is Karl König. At the age of sixteen, years before he ever heard of Steiner he went to his father, a deeply religious Jew, and said: "Father, I am a Christian." He knew that this confession was bound to hurt deeply the father whom he respected. During his whole life König referred to his Jewish descent.

The respectful silence in Camphill House while König was meditating evoked the ethos of the Viennese tradition of muted voices and eager anticipation among the Rabbinical pupils while their teacher was intent on prayer and clarification. *"Der Rebbe klärt,"* is a phrase from stories and anecdotes understood by non-Jews and Jews alike. The characteristic centre of Camphill life, the Bible evening, no doubt is largely based on Tilla König's experience in Herrenhut. But it has equally strong connections to the meal of Jewish tradition. König's biographer, Hans Müller-Wiedermann told me that for him writing this book arose out of his own deep striving for a new harmonization of German-Jewish relationships.

So I venture now to answer the question: Why should participants in the pre-natal school of St. Michael choose an incarnation in a Jewish surrounding? I admonish myself not to generalize for the ways of karma are most diverse and subtle. But it is my conviction that pupils of St. Michael in whose school, as Steiner tells us, the new Christianity formed the core of the "teaching" received could hardly have chosen a more direct way to the new Mysteries, the mysteries of Christ, than by spending their childhood and youth in a Jewish surrounding. Not only were they spared the ministrations of the traditional churches which caused in so many of our contemporaries indifference towards, and even contempt for Christianity, but in the Jews' concern for God and in their religious practice in daily life they acquired a basis for direct access to the Mystery of Golgotha and for a strong and individual religious life with or without a renewed Christian ritual. The Jew's endeavour to live his daily life as an act of devotion can lead directly to accept Steiner's challenge in the central meditation of the anthroposophist: "Practice, practice, practice."

# II

# What God Is—or Isn't

## A JEWISH WALDORF TEACHER'S VIEW

### BY SAMUEL ICHMANN

*from* INFO 3 *June 2000*

*translated by Judith Krischik*

WE'VE HEARD THE ACCUSATION regarding "anti-Semitism in Waldorf schools," but how does a Waldorf teacher with Jewish roots experience this? After decades of experience, he concludes that if we are to avoid the pitfalls of discrimination, we can hardly content ourselves with quoting anthroposophical tenets. Though there may be no anti-Jewish attitudes as such, cliché-ridden ideas about Judaism—whether as the product of traditional Christianity or of dogmatic over-interpretations of Steiner—have also surfaced in Waldorf schools.

To talk about being a Jew in Germany opens up a minefield! It immediately sets up snares and pitfalls: of nostalgic sentimentality, suppressed dialogue, the black hole of our response to the cruelty Germans practised on Jews, a feeling of resignation about the Shoah's destruction of hopes for a reunification of German and Jewish cultures. Above all, the enormous awkwardness this theme awakens. But beyond all the traps and difficulties, it is still a subject waiting for an answer, everything is still to be played out.

As a Jew living in Germany, in fact, I have also come to sense that here—and perhaps only here—we have reached such a "ground zero," such a *tabula rasa*, that a new beginning might actually be possible. The shock of the unimaginable, perhaps, has created a space where we might—and, in fact, must— approach this subject in a quite new and different way. The stigmata of disaster in the body of Germany's history mean that every straying from such a path leads straight to scandal. Could what is reported from contemporary Hungary ever happen here now—where in a football match in the Budapest stadium involving a club that Jews have supported as long as anyone can remember, hooligans on the other side started chanting: "Die, Jewish scum"? Or does such a thing not happen in Germany only because there isn't actually a football team supported by Jews, and because the majority of Germans have never even seen a "real live Jew"?

## A JEW IN THE WALDORF SCHOOL

Then again, what about this for a theme—to be a Jewish teacher in a Waldorf school, somewhere in Germany! Anyone interested? When someone works in education, do his roots matter, and does it matter what kind of beliefs and mentality he has developed as a result of his own upbringing and education? Isn't this kind of education, at least, something that stresses the humanity of human beings? Isn't it a pedagogy that lives in the perception of a dynamic spiritual core in every child? And anyway, don't its impulses merge seamlessly with the central truth of all humanity's religious traditions? Isn't the Waldorf school, as a place where striving people can meet—independent of race, nation, and religious or scientific persuasion—analogous with the basic principle that Steiner wished for members of the Anthroposophical Society? Isn't this true for teachers as well as pupils and parents? No doubt. Except that we do not live in an ahistorical vacuum of general principles, but in the concrete reality of actual situations and accrued, often unpondered, mentalities. Our ideals may be coherent and united, but life does not always look quite the same. Which is a good thing, for if this kind of education were a pre-packaged article it could not be what it is: ongoing task and living development.

## What Started Me Writing This?

This particular article was prompted by the steady stream of accusations about racism in Steiner's works and in Waldorf education. Rumors have surfaced recently of anti-Semitic discrimination said to have occurred in Waldorf schools—an explosive theme, at least in German-speaking countries. These rumors seem to have no basis in reality. And even if some individual teacher did go off the rails in this sense, one wouldn't necessarily be entitled to draw any conclusions about the general views of an entire pedagogical movement. It is clear that racism and anti-Semitism are completely at odds with the ethical foundations on which anthroposophical pedagogy rests. Anthroposophy is fairly inevitably exposed to slander, as a result of people's hazy perception of its different and demanding nature. In trying to awaken spiritual responsibility, it sometimes unleashes subconscious reactions. Naturally, the best way to test its usefulness and validity would be through conscious and considered scrutiny, but opponents seldom pursue this path. Thus it can stimulate irrational hatred—which, of course, puts it on a par with Judaism.

We must rebuff unfounded and distorted portrayals. I absolutely support those who reacted swiftly, energetically, and intelligently to insinuations recently broadcast on German television. Yet it is easy to overlook some internal perspectives; and it may be of some interest to hear what a Jew has to say who has been a Waldorf teacher in Germany for many years. Such a person could contribute two things as it were from the sidelines of such debate. First, he could show how Jewishness is sometimes perceived, could point out some very German symptoms—but also some that seem to be induced by a specifically anthroposophical response. Let me stress at the outset that this has nothing to do either with the nature of Germans or with that of anthroposophy as such, but ultimately with the fact that people are people, and that this is a very difficult issue. Secondly, he could try to show how in a Waldorf teacher—a German-speaking, Central European Jew—spiritual motifs from Judaism and anthroposophy meet in a way that has become important for him on his pedagogical path. This, for me, is really the point of this article. The circumstances I described were the immediate stimulus for me to further explore my own spiritual understanding, and I needed to share something of this, not to accuse or start a polemic. However, becoming aware of areas of unclarity in our relationship to anthroposophy should also be seen as a useful task. The aphoristic and anecdotal notes contained in what follows are unquestionably subjective. They do not by any means represent all that I might say on the subject of Waldorf education, anthroposophy, and Judaism, nor are they in any way conclusive or final. They represent only one aspect of my personal biographical experiences—though certainly not an unimportant one.

## "BUT YOU WON'T FORCE THAT DOWN EVERYONE'S THROATS, WILL YOU?"

I sit in a restaurant not far from an East European capital, opposite a fairly prominent German colleague, whom I hold in high regard. We have been brought together by a training project for Waldorf education, in which we are both teaching. The food is excellent and we take the opportunity to get better acquainted with each other. The conversation is open and friendly: we tell each other about our life and experience, exchange personal stories. At some point or other I "out" myself as a Jew. My colleague looks at me a little uncertainly and says: "But you won't force that down everyone's throats, will you?" I do not know what to reply. Does he mean something like "insist on telling everyone"? Is that what I have just done—unwittingly, or even with Jewish chutzpah? I examine myself. No, I do not have the tendency to

"embarrass" people by making them classify me immediately as a
Jew. On the other hand, I do not have the slightest inclination,
either, to keep it a secret. Why should I? Jews who keep quiet
about their Jewishness may have their own personal reasons (or
complexes), but this was never something I wanted to do. I have
always taken the opportunity of informing my colleagues about
this aspect of my origins whenever it seemed natural and sensible
to do so, as I did in this long conversation on a gentle summer's
evening, far away from Germany. So I'm at a loss for words now,
and my colleague also says nothing for a minute, then adds the
following question: "But you are a Christian surely?" This is
somewhat unexpected. What does he mean by this? He knows,
after all, that I am a dedicated Waldorf teacher, well-acquainted
for years with the foundations of anthroposophy. They are my
daily bread if I am serious about my profession. How could I
have elbowed out the important motifs of Christology? I have
also just been telling him about my involvement in religion teaching. Or was he not listening properly? What answer does he want
from me? Should I tell him of intimate experiences that every
pupil on a spiritual path is careful to keep to himself? I hesitate
for a fairly long moment. If I don't like keeping quiet about my
Jewishness, this applies even more so to my conviction about
Jesus of Nazareth as Messiah. Does he mean this question when
he uses the word "Christian"? I am not a Christian in the traditional sense: I have never left the Jewish community in which I
grew up, nor have I ever joined a Christian church. But he, as an
anthroposophist and Waldorf teacher, will surely not care about
that, or even expect otherwise! I reply to his question with a
thoughtful "Yes." I don't need to unsettle him, surely? Later, on
the way to my lodgings, I think about it all again and have mixed
feelings. Perhaps I should have unsettled him! Wouldn't it have
shown more presence of mind to answer with Kierkegaard's great
phrase: "One cannot be a Christian, only become one"?

I tell this anecdote because it highlights a deep problem.
Taking aside all over-hasty labels, identifications, "isms" and

ideologies, what do people really know about the way Jews look at the world? What do they know of the feeling of opposition, often only resonating in unspoken, subconscious realms, to having any kind of idolatry forced on one? Of the one and one-half millennia of reservation about a Christianity that, through many of its representatives as well as many of the forms of worship and doctrine it assumed, could not—and was not permitted to—answer Jewish needs; of the inner strength and warmth that it draws from the spirituality of its traditions, and that it is a strange blindness to want to deprive it of—for until late in the twentieth century, only by being so deprived was a Jew allowed to be accepted as a Christian; of the impossibility of regarding as obsolete, superfluous, and redundant things of the most intimate, personal, profound meaning that one drank in, as it were, at one's mother's breast—because, once "Christ had appeared," all this was apparently no longer valid!

I don't really want to plunge into theological debate at this point, but one thing is certain: Christians who ponder their outlook and roots are very aware nowadays that to deny Judaism is to undermine their own origins. But it is this same misguided tradition of denial, reaching far back to the first centuries of the post-Christian era, and extending into our own recent past, that has sometimes worked its way into people's (mis)conceptions of anthroposophy and Waldorf education. But this rests on the projection of what I believe are wholly false interpretations onto Steiner's Christology, on the continued circulation of theological prejudices that were at least partly overcome after the Second World War, though not necessarily in our circles.

## DON'T READ "ENGRAVED IN STONE," READ "FREEDOM"

I look back on myself in my early years as a Waldorf teacher—almost thirty years ago—sitting in the college meeting of a south German Waldorf school, where I completed my apprenticeship. I also look back with much gratitude to the dear colleague of mine whom I am about to quote. I met him again a few years ago, and thanked him for the many helpful personal conversations we had. He is a very modest person who never said anything without reflecting on it first, and never adopted a "holier than thou" attitude. The words that I am about to cite undoubtedly, therefore, expressed a genuine conviction that he, a scientist, drew from the general mood that still held sway then in Waldorf education as a relic from the pre-war years. "Judaism," he said, "is purely a religion of laws. Even today a strictly orthodox Jewish doctor would still be forbidden to heal someone who is near death on the Sabbath." We had been talking about Jesus' healings on the Sabbath as described in the Gospels. I must stress that there wasn't the slightest nuance of disdain or even anti-Semitism in his words or his attitude. He simply put it forward as a fact of cultural history. And was not contradicted. Not even by me. In my own defense, I can say that I—very young, and sitting there among tried and tested, experienced authorities—was at first distressed, for I had never heard such a thing before, and it seemed to me to be diametrically opposed to the Jewish ethos of "he who saves a single person, saves the whole world." Secondly, I had grown up in a religious but not an orthodox context, and was not very knowledgeable on questions of *halachah*, or interpretation of the ritual laws.

Thirdly, the discussion had moved on to another point before I had regained my inner focus. Nevertheless, this and other similar situations were a stimulus for me to broaden and deepen my knowledge of Judaism. In brief, the above statement about not saving someone on the Sabbath is false: according to religious laws, a doctor is actually obliged to try and help a sick person who is close to death, on the Sabbath or otherwise. But even the more general assertion that the Jewish religion is one based only on laws turns out on closer inspection to be rather inaccurate. I am not disputing that there are fossilized forms of religious observance. But the real sense of the *mitzvot*—an untranslatable word that is often rendered as "duties"—is linked with one of the deepest spiritual attitudes toward the world that we know in all religious history: the consecration of every action, even the slightest and smallest—in other words, deed as prayer.

In Hasidism this tendency blossomed in great and undogmatic fashion. The essence of *mitzvot* enters a class-teacher's activity each day if he teaches with moral intuition and imagination. There is also a wonderful Talmudic phrase that belongs here, that bursts from within the confines of purely legalistic understanding that people like to foist on Judaism. It arises through a kind of play on words, which has a fairly important role in traditional Bible interpretation. Because the Hebrew script has consonants only, a word in the Torah can receive various different meanings according to the vowels one gives it. The passage in Exodus to which I am referring relates to the tables of the law, in which the so-called ten commandments (actually, the "ten words") were engraved. The sentence goes: *Al tigra harut ela herut*, which in translation is: "Don't read 'engraved in stone,' read 'freedom'." I recommend this as a meditation for those who wish to ponder the spirit of the Torah, and perhaps for others as well—it might prove a useful approach, for instance, to interpreting the Waldorf curriculum. Or for "reading" another human being, for thinking deeply about a child's nature and trying to conjure up his or her past and future development before our inner eyes.

## JEWISH CARICATURE

I cannot continue my account without speaking of the Oberufer *Three Kings' Play* that is often performed in Waldorf schools. As people may know, unlike the other two Oberufer plays—the *Paradise* and the *Shepherds'* plays—the clergy had a hand in creating this highly dramatic piece of folk theatre, and it is perhaps for this reason that the priests and high priests were given the general gloss of "Jews." Was this an attempt to hide the fact that every cleric, even a Christian one, can sometimes act more as a hindrance to, rather than a mediator of, good? Or was it a straight-forward reference to the Jews as "God-murderers"? Whatever the truth, I would like to describe the impression made on me the first time I saw the *Three Kings' Play.* This was at the Uhlandshöhe Waldorf School in Stuttgart, in 1973. I stress the date because I assume that things have changed since then, and that the play is no longer directed there in the same way. I was attending the Stuttgart Waldorf teacher-training course at the time, and we students were invited to see the plays.

The play struck me as a powerful and remarkable piece of theater, with an intense inwardness that greatly appealed to me, and which I gladly involved myself in—and then the "Jews" appeared all of a sudden. They wore East European Orthodox Jewish costume—broad-rimmed black hats, caftans, beards and long sidelocks—and twitched, pitter-pattered about, spoke in a hasty, fidgety jargon, and finally fell over backward together off their bench. This was, by the way, quite a theatrical achievement, for the teachers were not professional actors. One can imagine the uproarious laughter of a hall full of children of all ages. But I was deeply troubled. Oversensitive reaction from someone who still bore the wounds that a collective memory retained from centuries of persecution and denigration? Or quite simply the fact that my great-grandfather on my mother's side, Israel Schuchner, used to wear such a costume, and he was a quiet, pious man devoted to prayer and study of the Torah, who had the good fortune to die a natural death shortly before the Nazis arrived in the East European town where he lived? (My great-grandmother, Perl Rochel, was transported to Auschwitz at over age eighty, together with some of her children and grandchildren. None of them returned.) But perhaps my distress was also connected with everyone's unexpressed awkwardness about such things.

At the school where I first taught as a Waldorf teacher, I was asked to join the "Three Kings' company" barely a year later. The director, someone for whom I had and still have the greatest respect, and who sadly died far too young, was a Waldorf teacher of the "old guard," son of a teacher on the very first college of teachers of 1919. He knew of my Jewish origins and thought I might, for that very reason, be able to bring an authentic quality to the gestures! At the time I was astonished at this German naivete, and am still astonished today. Luckily, the costumes at this school were quite different from the ones in Stuttgart—very original, stylized priest costumes, without the faintest resemblance to village Jews of Eastern and Central Europe. I also noticed that for these characters the term "high priests" gradually replaced the designation "Jews"; and I remember a colleague asking the striking question in a college meeting whether, after what the Germans had done to the Jews, one ought still to perform this play at all. It is only in retrospect I realize that in the early seventies the process of working through recent German history had really only just begun. However, I did not accept the role offered me (taking another instead).

## WHAT GOD IS—OR ISN'T

I would like to relate one further symptomatic tale. We are now no longer in southern Germany but in the north. Here a fresh wind blows, people are more tolerant, more open, and have more distance from things than in the south. I have returned to Germany after a longish time working in another European country—in the year, when neo-Nazis were setting houses and people on fire—and my homecoming is not altogether encouraging. A few more grey hairs, rather fewer illusions, but by no means burned out.

We, teachers of nondenominational religion lessons, are sitting in the school library together with a Christian Community priest. We are studying a theme from Christology. The invited priest takes part in the discussion, contributing very clear formulations. As things unfold, the north-German priest—a cultivated figure, very well-educated and doubtless profoundly knowledgeable about esoteric themes—says with powerful conviction and in a tone of forceful pronouncement: "Yahweh is not the Father God!" He, by the way, is unaware of my Jewish ancestry.

This contemplative meeting is not the right place for an argument, and I am not much interested, anyway, in hammering out questions of religious dogma. I know of Steiner's great teachings of cosmology and divine hierarchy, and of the specific perspectives derived from occult research, and regard it as an important task to integrate these with my knowledge and understanding. Various studies of my own have also given me some familiarity with the patristic and Scholastic fields, as well as with some basic aspects of church council and heretic history, with their disputes over dogma. The question of the Trinity has occupied me for a long time—not only as an academic, historical question, but also as a living one, and naturally, too, in relation to Steiner's pedagogical anthropology, which refers to a trinity within the human being and the world. I try to connect with experiences and insights such as those evoked by the 1923/24 Foundation Stone meditation, seeking to avoid speculations in which the intellect assumes it "knows what's what" as far as divinity is concerned.

"Yahweh is not the Father God"! I go home, and this "is not" refuses to let go of me. What troubles me, somehow, is not the content but the way it was put, not the question but the apodictic "thus it is." I naturally respect the fact that a priest preaches—that's his job, after all. Maybe he doesn't have to do it everywhere, all the time, but we all have our human failings. Yet what am I meant to make of this "is not"? I want to find out what it is that bothers me about it. Is it really the way it was said, or perhaps the content, after all? I decide to make full use of the school library where this discussion took place over the next few days, for it contains a complete edition of Rudolf Steiner's works. With the aid of an index and reference volume I examine every passage I can find in which Steiner said anything about the being of Yahweh. Naturally I cannot cite chapter and verse here, but as I read it becomes very clear to me that it is impossible to derive an ultimate "is" or "is not" from the dynamic, descriptive depiction characteristic of Steiner. He approaches this, as many other questions, from the most varied perspectives; and the student only arrives at a fuller understanding, beyond Steiner's actual text, by combining these perspectives! But maybe this is my Jewish mentality coming to the fore again—"Don't read 'engraved in stone,' read 'freedom'"!—that does not wish to pigeon-hole the spiritual and divine in the form of dogma and parroted phrases fixed by decree and made obligatory for believers.

Rabbinical Judaism, after all, contains the principle of *mahloqet*—or "multiplicity of voices"—in which different, conflicting teachings can stand alongside one another without being resolved. Perhaps the multiplicity of perspectives in Rudolf Steiner's work is also a kind of spiritual-scientific *mahloqet*?

Then something else of great importance also enters my reflections. I imagine someone going to a pious Jew and trying to explain to him that the divinity to which he prays daily is not the Father at all, the Creator, the Ground of Creation, Sustainer of the World, but "only"—well, whatever you like. He would shake his head at best—and rightly so. Who are we to fiddle around with the great traditions from outside, or to come along with our tuppence worth of academic learning? Thinking one knows better than others does not, as far as I am aware, belong to the virtues that Steiner recommended to those striving for knowledge.

A Jewish prayer book lies before me. Morning, afternoon, evening prayers: all imbued with the most solemn, sublime formulations, symbols and metaphors, which direct the praying person to ponder ultimate, absolute things; and all penetrated by the name of the Father. In the Passover Haggadah stand phrases that render any reductionism to "merely" hierarchical aspects impossible, though the latter do not, of course, have to be excluded. Even intertrinitarian differentiations, however important these may be in other contexts, have no place here, since they come, as one says in Jewish tradition, from "Greek," not Hebrew, thought.

And this "Hebrew" thinking, if you don't mind me saying so, has nothing to do with what people sometimes dismiss as "superseded," "abstract," and "monotheistic." "Greek" thinking, from Dionysus the Areopagite to Vladimir Soloviev, has its own inimitable flavor, its grandeur, beauty, and deep truth. But why should it be the only kind to approach Christ? A religion can, after all, only be understood from within, however difficult such a phenomenological methodology may be in practice. If I try to understand Buddhism through the views of Thomas Aquinas I have failed before I begin. And the reverse is also true, of course. In Christianity, naturally, people have got used to regarding Judaism as a mere preparatory stage, just as Judaism has come to see Christianity as a kind of apostasy. Nowadays, I believe, it is high time to overcome such habits of thought. Let me quote a passage from the Haggadah:

> I led you out of Egypt,
> not an angel
> and not a seraph
> and not a messenger.
> it was I Myself and no other.

Franz Rosenzweig, the great Jewish religious philosopher, articulated his understanding of the Messiah through this "I Myself and no other," and was the same man who once, in referring to the Jews' awaiting of the Messiah and the New Testament teaching of Christ's second coming, asked the enigmatic question whether, if these events should occur, they would not be one and the same!

## THE BREATH OF LEARNING CHILDREN

I remember in my student days how a French Christian Community priest once embraced me joyfully and told me how great was his love and reverence for Judaism. This heartfelt warmth was surely genuine. I once gave him a volume of Martin Buber's *Tales of the Hasidim*, and he later told me this was something all priests should read, and that it had been of great help to him in his work. A few years ago I also learned that Rudolf Steiner advised a young man who came to him to ask whether he should become a priest, to study the book of the Baal Shem Tov, the semi-legendary, eighteenth-century founder of the Hassidic movement. The question I have is whether this book might not be a very good resource for preparing for the "holy" profession of teacher, as Rudolf Steiner saw it.

It is increasingly hard to find access to impulses of thought and feeling that stress the religious quality of Waldorf education. In my opinion, this is not only because of the more-than-necessary compromises that have sometimes been internalized in people's feeling life, and stifle the spontaneity of our pedagogy; but because our desert wanderings doubtless have a purpose: to ignite an inner fire, one fed through the meeting of individuals. The deeper purpose of meeting is to practice attentiveness and devotion toward the being and potential of another, to the child made in the image of God who has been entrusted to me.

If I ponder—and I would like to conclude with this—the central task of education, particularly in our day and age, I think of that "learning to breathe," to which Rudolf Steiner gives such emphatic importance at the beginning of his *Study of Man*.[1] Are we really serious about this? Are we not frequently so out-of-breath ourselves in our daily rush that, while we understand this theoretically, and can relate all kinds of ideas to it, we do not in fact manage to make it real? Do we not need to daily recreate and revitalize our awareness of this in the most mundane of everyday situations? How strangely familiar and at the same time newly expressed for us is that Talmudic phrase that seems to have an inner relation to the underlying pedagogical and therapeutic motifs of Waldorf education, and is nevertheless coined in inimitable "Hebraic" manner: The world rests on the breath of learning children.

---

1. Available as *The Foundations of Human Experience*, Anthroposophic Press, 1996.

# 12

# The Dark Side of the Enlightenment

## The Eighteenth Century, Changing Perception of the World, and Anti-Semitism in the Early Modern Age

by Ralf Sonnenberg

*from* Die Drei *July 8, 2000*
*translated and abridged by Mado Spiegler*

## Summary

The Age of Enlightenment was shaped by the attempt to reduce reality to empirical laws, as well as to classify individuals according to one-sided theological categories. One example of that form of thought can be found in the treatment of Judaism.

## Medieval Perception of the World

The concept of enlightenment born in the eighteenth century described the dominant spiritual streams of the time, which saw the breakdown of the image of the world characteristic of the Christian Middle Ages. A simplified account of European Christians' spiritual experience before the age of great discoveries would go something like this: while wars, famines, epidemics, physical problems, or mystical anxieties often served to undermine human beings' sense of feeling at home in the world, they also felt that they were images of a meaningful cosmos, whose perceptible parts were themselves "meaning-bearers" of a higher totality. The medieval theologians and poets imagined the microcosm in the form of a human being whose very form represented the universe. Especially during the early and high Middle Ages, the analogy between human being and cosmos could be found everywhere—in philosophical *Summae*, chronicles, encyclopedias, and so on. Each region of the body corresponded to a region or an element of the physical universe (head=firmament; chest = air; belly = sea; legs = earth; bones=stones; arteries=branches; hair=grass; feelings=animals; etc. The body was part of the earth: its blood, water; its breath, air; its warmth, fire.).

Over the last few years, readers might have noticed an image, frequently reproduced on record labels and various catalogues of Hildegard of Bingen's songs. It shows a circle whose center is occupied by a man with arms extended. Just as a mother tenderly embraces her baby to protect it from the cold and harm, so here the earthly creature is protectively embraced by a trinitarian divinity of three anthropomorphic beings. Alan de Lisle tells us that, "All creatures on Earth are for us like a book, a mirror." People attempting to decipher the symbols hidden in the universe experienced themselves as the crown of the universe, the crown of creation, made in God's image. Whereas, by the Renaissance, a similar perception entailed a sense of complete human autonomy, the understanding conveyed by medieval cosmologies did not grant the human being a completely independent existence. Human beings had been made for the greater glory of the divinity, their yearnings for freedom and autonomy mediated through church institutions and biblical traditions.

This worldview rooted feelings and drives in a particular configuration of soul and spirit quite different from the modern disposition. The intensity with which medieval poetry, theology, and art keep returning to the theme of anthropomorphic nature and cosmic humanity are not simply a tribute to a tradition, or mere convention, but the expression of a very special relationship of the human being with nature, which has since disappeared. The unity between humankind and God, nature and cosmos, whose echo is still perceptible more or less clearly among some of our contemporaries, belonged to the common experiential fund of premodern culture, whose specific contents we now have difficulty imagining.

## THE BIRTH OF THE MODERN EXPERIENCE OF THE WORLD

One can only understand the Enlightenment in its many political, scientific, and literary aspects in the historical context of successive changes in self-perception and world-perception from Medieval to early modern times. In these changes, Italy and France played a pioneering role in the eleventh century. One of the main characteristics of this oft-described metamorphosis was the gradual formation and consolidation of individuality, accompanied by a gradual loss of the collective sense of embeddedness in the world as one's home, although the consequences of this discontinuity were not at first very visible. The excitement derived from the discovery and use of new capacities of soul and spirit, as well as resultant achievements in the realms of science, art, and technology, made it easy to remain unaware of the one-sidedness and dangers of this process. Fourteenth- to fifteenth-century humanism, marked by the awareness of a newly rediscovered antiquity, the rejection of authority, and the empirical sense of late Medieval society, provided the ferment that allowed the ideas and postulates of the Enlightenment to take over.

When we talk about the European Enlightenment, we are talking primarily of an intellectual movement centered in the seventeenth century,[1] with some overlaps into the sixteenth and eighteenth centuries, and with slightly different emphases in various European regions. In Great Britain, the term

---

1. The author expands here on a common view of the Enlightenment as an eighteenth-century phenomenon, and legitimately includes what is often designated these days as Early Modernity, where the Enlightenment is of course rooted. [trans. note]

Enlightenment was primarily applied to issues of political sovereignty and constitutions; the French were more focused on social issues. In Germany, the focus was on religious issues with an emphasis on ecclesiastic intolerance, superstition, the need for popular education, and legal justice.

As to the philosophical and ethical contents of Enlightenment, this was a matter of heated discussions among theologians, philosophers, and writers in the few decades preceding the French Revolution. For Immanuel Kant, enlightenment meant the "human departure from self-inflicted dependency."[2] *Sapere aude!* Dare to know! Human culture should no longer be determined by superstitious faith, but should look instead to the goddess Reason for direction. Both in English and in French, the word "enlightenment" still carried some of the connotations of the Medieval light-metaphors that pointed to the higher source of *intelligentia,* which was recruited to serve the conquest of the sensory world.[3] The confidence and the sense of almost unlimited "knowability" of the sensory world opened the way to an optimistic faith in progress that extended deep into the twentieth century.

If we inquire about the causes and context of this historical phenomenon, a few things immediately strike us as symptoms of deeper spiritual transformations. Religious wars between Christian confessions played an important role in this change. Together with the loss of ecclesiastical authority came the discovery of modern "natural law" and natural rights. The *lex naturalis* looked to the personal realm as an autonomous sphere of rights that must be protected from authoritarian abuses. Natural law turned away from a divine origin as the source of rulership, governmental forms, and social structures, finding instead their origin and ground in free, equal human beings.

---

2. Immanuel Kant in *Berlinische Monatsschrift* 2, 1783, p. 481.
3. Cf. also Rudolf Steiner, GA 26, *Anthroposophische Leitsätze,* pp. 59–68.

The transformation from pre-modern holistic cosmologies to a factual consciousness was linked to the replacement of the Ptolemaic Earth-centered universe by the heliocentric picture of the world, accompanied by the disappearance of a sense of spiritual connections between human lives, the physical Earth, and other planets. Very soon, the divine hierarchies that used to rule the movements of the planets were replaced by physical laws with mathematical underpinnings. The Platonic conception of a *scala naturae*, as it had lived in the Middle Ages and into the Renaissance, was replaced by a mechanistic description of nature. Medicine started looking at human beings as just one species among others, so that the doctor's analytical view of the unique difference between ensouled humans and animals became increasingly questionable. The image of the human being as the crown of creation was replaced by a sense that human beings could know the world more and more completely, and some day rule it entirely.

## THE RELATIONSHIP BETWEEN JUDAISM AND CHRISTIANITY

This new empirical view of humanity and history was not problem-free, as is clear from the evolution of the view of Judaism in eighteenth-century literature. The image of the Jews fostered by the Enlightenment and Romantic idealism was marked by many ambivalences, between demands for freedom and equality for the followers of all religions, and horrified fascination with the alien and completely Other. [4]

The most notable representatives of the Jewish-Christian Enlightenment were Moses Mendelssohn and Gotthold Ephraim Lessing. For them, only the renunciation of tradition

---

4. See Urs Bitterli, *Die Wilden und die Zivilisierten. Grundzüge einer Geistes– und Kulturgeschichte eüropäisch–überseeischen Begegnunge*, Munich, 1991.

and connections inherited from the past could lead to a true knowledge of the divine and make it possible for human beings to overcome the mutual alienation induced by the artificial distinctions between religions. While Lessing pleaded for a purification of Christianity from all "irrational elements," such as the belief in biblical miracles and the supernatural nature of Jesus, and the replacing of official Christianity with a religion of reason, Mendelssohn's efforts aimed at the "removal of all mythical and superstitious ceremonies and usages" from Jewish religion. In his famous "Philosophical Talks" in 1775, Mendelssohn argued for emancipation from the Medieval "ghetto-mentality" and the full integration of the Jewish minority into Christian societies. Coming from a more secular point of view, Wilhelm von Dohm, the Prussian secretary of war, published his *On the Civic Improvement of the Jews* (1781) in which he denounced the historical and cultural position of the Jews and called for thorough reforms, granting German Jews full civic rights in exchange for assuming all the responsibilities of citizenship in a modern state. In exchange, he called upon the Jews to renounce all religious connections and institutions in order to become loyal representatives of the Prussian Commonwealth (*Staatswesen*). In other words, legal equality was predicated on the Jews' readiness to become completely assimilated.[5] As a laconic Heine was to remark later, Christian baptism would be the "ticket" allowing the formerly downtrodden and segregated Jews to enter middle-class civic society. However, any readiness for tolerance on the part of Christian authors and politicians ended the minute members of a minority religion asked for the right to retain their cultural identity. Thus there were, as the sociologist Detlev Classen remarks, impassable "boundaries of Enlightenment" which would pave the way for political and ideological

---

5. Christian Wilhelm Dohm, *Uber die bürgerliche Verbesserung der Juden* 1781-1783.

modern anti-Semitism.[6] Some of the "Enlighteners" opposed Jewish emancipation, arguing that they were religiously and biologically unable to assume civic rights and duties. Thus the Goettingen professor of theology Johann David Michaelis, who was sure that the Jews' nature was completely unalterable, gave scientific form to Medieval ideas of the Jews' stubborn hearts, which until then had been almost exclusively embedded in religious controversies.

## Anti-Judaism in German Romanticism and in Fichte and Hegel's Idealism

One of the most notable mediators between the Enlightenment notions of universalism and the early-Romantic fondness for folk themes was Johann Gottfried Herder, whose 1791 *Philosophical History of Humanity* lay the groundwork for an idea of national psychologies rooted in cosmological considerations that attributed successive cultural epochs and various European ethnic groups with more or less equal positions within planetary schemes. He formulated a "triadic" philosophy of history in which one could see the first lineaments of modern evolutionary theories, although it was to be another ten years before an attempt was made to design a "scientific" classification of human races and families. This was first attempted between 1801 and 1805, when Johann Friedrich Reitenmeier's *History of the Prussian States* endeavored to demonstrate the Slavs' natural inferiority. It must be pointed out that Reitenmeier was crossing a bridge there that Herder had avoided: Herder's general overview of all ethnic groups still saw all individual peoples as equal materializations of God's thought. The separation of spirit and nature was, in Herder's work, transcended by his pantheism, for he saw all of nature as born of the spirit and

---

6. Detlev Classen, *Grenzen der Aufklärung. Die gesellschaftliche Genese des modernen Antisemitismus*, Frankfurt a/M, 1994.

penetrated by spirit. Peoples and cultures, therefore, were organisms in which an evolutionary principle was concretely revealed. In his panorama of human history, individual cultures and races constituted a many-membered whole, which the author compared to the variety of plants growing in God's great garden. History, for Herder, was the workshop of super-sensible forces whose metamorphoses determined successive historical manifestations.

At the same time, Herder's views on "the people of the Old Testament" were quite ambivalent, in a way that was not, of course, unusual for its time. In 1782, in his *On the Spirit of Hebraic Poetry*, a speaker indefatigably defended the Jews against a whole range of negative judgments. The author expressed his conviction that the Jews had a specific "Spirit," a folk-individuality that was one facet of the divine truth.[7] For many years, Herder's work was considered the foundation of all thinking about the Old Testament, and a touchstone of Christian histories of the Hebrew Scriptures.

A diametrically opposed view was taken in Herder's other book, *Ideen*, whose cosmopolitan intentions are unquestionable.[8] There, he acknowledged the divine character of Mosaic Law, which is the foundation of Jewish religion, and even seemed to defend its transmission against the attacks of "alien, contemptuous enemies of the Jews." At the same time, the book described the Jewish people as having been involved in an unremitting and irreversible downfall, starting with the completion of Solomon's Temple. Herder claimed that ever since that time, Jewish religion had been made "despicable and ridiculous to other nations" by the Pharisees' "obsession with nitpicking wordplay," their "literalism," and their patrio-

7. Johann Gottfried Herder, *Vom Geist der hebräischen Poesie*, in *Sämtliche Werke*, Stuttgart, 1852, vol. I, 211 ff.
8. J.G. Herder, *Ideen zur Philosophie der Geschichte der Menschheit*, Bodenheim, 1995, p. 312.

tism, which was merely a "slavish dependency... on outdated laws."

Furthermore, Herder held the Jews responsible for the paralysis and stagnation of Western natural science and historiography, for they had transmitted to the rest of humanity (superstitious) myths like the forty-day flood, or the idea of Daniel's four monarchies. He neglected to mention, of course, that other writers were making precisely the same argument about aspects of the Christian New Testament.

Whatever the case might be, Herder was sure that the single obstacle to the proper evolution of the West had been the survival of the "Hebrew spirit" beyond its proper time. As far as he was concerned, centuries of Jewish influence had paralyzed the evolution of morality and political institutions: the Hebrew Bible's misunderstanding of the spirit of nations had stopped the development of humanity. Using the faulty (Jewish) model of a religion incarnated in a state, the modern states were imprisoning free Christianity—whose nature was purely moral—in the rigid corset of state religions.

Of course, Herder's critique of Jewish spiritual life was also an attack against the Christian establishment, whose representatives were trying to stop the development of the natural sciences and the dawning of a renewed, free Christianity. Interestingly, however, Herder did not envisage the absorption of the Jews into this future renewed Christianity, having instead assigned the Jewish diaspora a useful function in the strictly economic sphere. This went with Herder's conviction that "the people of God, to whom God himself had given them their land thousands of years ago," had somehow perversely chosen to be "a parasite in other nations," rather than demanding their own land back as would have been suggested by a sense of honor and a natural desire for a home. That in the age of Romantic nations, the Jews did not have a nation of their own was perceived by Herder as an affront against the divine plan for humanity (presumably in strong contradistinction to the Germans' then-powerful nostalgia for an end to the disintegration of their own nation into hundreds of little feudal states).

The transition from this "enlightened" anti-Judaism to a modern anti-Semitism based on racist biology was fairly smooth. In 1793, Fichte accused the Jews of forming "a state within the state," supposedly as a matter of free choice, whereas in reality their segregation in a group subject to its own laws was the result of state impositions. The only solution, for Fichte, short of "cutting off all their heads and replacing them with heads in which there wouldn't be a single Jewish idea" (obviously a somewhat unfeasible solution) was to "reconquer their beloved Palestine for them and send them all back home." Fichte later became a member of a "Christian-German" organization that had many prominent members, and from which converted Jews and their descendants were strictly excluded.

A similarly vacillating position could be found in Hegel's writings. Like Herder, he saw a place—indeed an important place—for Jews in the unfolding of history. But having failed to follow Jesus, they had chosen to stay in front of the door, and, not surprisingly, were being oppressed as a result; they had, as it were, stepped off the majestic train of history. If they had not accepted Christ, it must be because of some deep-seated incapacity to do so: "The lion cannot fit into a nut—the infinite spirit has not room enough in the prison-cell of a Jewish soul."[9] At other times, Hegel and many other authors attributed Jewish limitations to the fact that they renounced having a nation of their own. This somehow made them examples of what Kant described as humanity's "self-inflicted dependency."[10]

9. Johann Friedrich Wilhelm Hegel, *Phänomenologie des Geistes*, Hamburg, 1952, p. 250; and H. Nohl (ed.), *Hegels theologische Jugendschriften*, Frankfurt, 1966, p. 312.
10. J. G. Fichte, *Sämtliche Werke*, Berlin, 1845, vol. VI, p. 149 ff.

All these thinkers were following the trail of an old Christian tradition according to which Jewish religion had become obsolete as a result of Christ's incarnation. If the Old Testament merely existed as a preparation for the New Testament, it seemed logical to think that the Jews were somehow "left behind" by the evolution of humanity. For Schelling, Catholicism and Protestantism were both stages on the path to the final revelation based on St. John's *Apocalypse,* in which the universal myth of reason and Christian religion would be at last reunited. This future "Christendom of Reason" was, for Schelling, the highest stage of the evolution of the Trinity. Christ would return, having assumed some of the features of a triumphant Dionysus, and open the new age of a free humanity, thus ending the rule of the "Jewish spirit of unfreedom."[11]

To the very extent that Christianity was descended from Judaism and "fulfilled" its prophecies, the Jews supposedly had no more reason to exist. While this belief had survived through the centuries and made it difficult to see the Jews objectively, it became even harder by the end of the nineteenth century, once these views had been encrusted in an "objective," "modern" worldview, part of a modern philosophy that prided itself on its freedom from superstition. Anti-Semitic themes inherited from the hegemony of Christian civilization in Europe now became ascribed to scientific-minded modernity inspired by dreams of universalism and freedom.

---

11. Friedrich Schelling, *Philosophie der Offenbarung* (1841), Frankfurt, 1977, p. 322 ff.

# 13

# François Joseph Molitor's Philosophy of History
## Judaism as the Miniature Reflection of Humanity

BY János Darvas

*from* Info 3, *December* 2000

*translated and excerpted by Mado Spiegler*

Only slowly are cliches and prejudices being cleared away from our conventional representations about Judaism. In the mid-nineteenth century, the forgotten scholar François Joseph Molitor initiated this trend: his appreciation of the past, present, and future of Judaism remains relevant today.

### Portrait of a Bridge Builder and a Discovery

One of the most noticeable phenomena in the theology of the past fifty years is an interest in the Jewish roots of Christianity. Catholics, Protestants, and even the more progressive representatives of Russian Orthodoxy, are increasingly surprised by the depth of the Jewish roots in the actions and sayings of Jesus and his apostles. Commonplace prejudices are being revised and rethought by mainstream theology. The role of Judaism in the origins of Christianity is no longer taken for granted. We can now see as unfounded propaganda excesses like the construction of an "Aryan" Jesus (which is quite common in the right wing of the political spectrum, and was not invented by Hitler). The boundary between Christianity and Judaism, which had seemed immutable for several centuries, is currently being re-thought.

This boundary was always a "forced" one (distinguishing as it did between a "true religion of freedom" and a somewhat inferior religion "based on law." New paths are being sought on the Christian side, out of a feeling that faith needs to be renewed by a return to roots. Until now, an insistence on differences, real or imagined, was considered necessary to the defense of one's own side.

## CHRISTIAN THEOLOGY'S CHANGE OF DIRECTION

With the exception of a few sentimental excesses, the change of direction over the last ten years must be noted as a sign of a growing self-confidence: an end of theological bidding wars, and an end to the overemphasis on the self (not a very Christian attitude). "Do not raise yourself above the other branches. You may brag, but you do not bear the root. The root bears you," as it says in Paul's letters to the Romans (Rom. I:11,18), where he mentions the eternal validity of Jewish chosenness.

If, instead of defensively improving my position by demeaning others, I can constructively assert myself in relation to another—especially one who shares my origins and destiny—the result is a very productive situation; evolution takes place. The Catholic theologian Verena Lenzen conducts her research on a central and difficult theme in Jewish existence, *Kidush HaShem* (the blessing of the Holy Name) by slipping into the skin of Judaism, entering Jewish assumptions.[1]

Her research and that of others is not obsessed with the desire to level everything, or to erase all religious divergences. Rather, it is a new perception and understanding. A third way

---

1. Verena Lenzen, *Jüdisches Leben und Sterben im Namen Gottes—Studien über die Heiligung des göttlichen Namens.* Munich, 1995.

is being opened between a dead science of religion—abstract, apparently neutral, and academic on one hand, and on the other hand, a defensive self-justification inspired by ideological positioning and apologetics. This requires a virtue of attention, which is not sufficiently summarized by the words "tolerance" or "open-mindedness." I personally would prefer the word "acknowledgment," which seems more accurate. Acknowledgment is more than simple tolerance, for the latter does not demand that we enter into a relation with the essence and difference of the other; all that is required is the recognition of a general right to existence granted to the one we "tolerate." Acknowledging means active attentiveness, the encouragement and support of that which is unique in the other. This is a good occasion to remember Goethe's saying, unfortunately not followed enough: "In truth, tolerance can only be a temporary condition. It must lead to a full acknowledgment. To tolerate in the sense of enduring is an affront."[2]

## Christian Anti-Judaism

The evolution I just underlined is relatively recent. It had some precursors, but it did not become anchored in the wider public—at least the more educated public—until the abomination of the Holocaust forced even the elites of the church into a radical rethinking.

At present, we are discovering new aspects that run counter to almost two thousand years of old ways of thinking and feeling. These antiquated conceptions, widespread enough to have become part of the "habitus" of many Christian nations and cultures, left deep and tragic cultural remnants in their wake.

As a result of the incarnation of Christ in Jesus Christ, the place of the Jewish people as the chosen people became obsolete. The role of "chosen" was now assigned to the Christian

---

2. J.W. Goethe, *Maxims and Reflections*.

church, the "New Israel." It was located in the church, the body
of Christ. Thus the Jews' mission was ended. Popular versions
of this doctrine even consider the Jewish people to be excluded
altogether from the divine plan of salvation. The totality of the
Jewish nation is expected to assume responsibility for the death
of Christ. These ideas, presented as "facts" of the history of
salvation, have deep consequences. Those Jews who refused to
"give up" were collectively discriminated against as being
"murderers of God," and discrimination was carried into the
legal and economic realms. This doctrine of the Jews as "dei-
cides" was even incorporated into the liturgy of Good Friday,
and it wasn't until Pope John XXIII that these references were
eliminated from the liturgy of the Mass. The most important
texts in the New Testament referring to the history of salvation
announce, in vigorously expressive images, the irreversible election of the Jewish people; despite this, chapters nine to eleven
in Paul's letter to the Romans were omitted, diverted, or misin-
terpreted, with effects that can hardly be overestimated. Alienation and hostility became permanent features between
Christians and Jews, spreading over the whole Western world
from late antiquity to modern times. The chasm created
between pagan peoples only superficially Christianized and the
immemorial traditions of the Jews is one of the indicators of
the tragedy of historical Christianity. (…)

Of the many authorities of the universal doctrine, only a very
few, like Vladimir Soloviev, were able to break the unreflective
anti-Judaic consensus and seek a path that would restore to
Judaism a function based not on any kind of "tolerance," but
on the acknowledgment of its specific role in the concert of
world religions. The fundamental recasting of thought has only
just begun.[3]

---

3. For the persistence of these attitudes in anthroposophical milieus, see Samuel Ichmann, *Was Gott ist… oder auch nicht. Aufzeichnungen eines jüdischen Waldorflehrers,*
*Info3,* June 2000. Translated in this volume. chapter 11.

## FRANÇOIS JOSEPH MOLITOR — A DISCOVERY

It seems appropriate to call attention to a great unknown of the German Idealist movement who embarked on an exploration of the heart of mystical Judaism, and built theological bridges on the basis of an intimate knowledge of Jewish tradition. He is also a shining representative of the "Judeo-German symbiosis," which was to founder with the advent of National Socialism.

The man is François Joseph Molitor (1779-1860), born in Oberursel, near Frankfurt—author of *Philosophy of History or of Tradition in the Old Testament and Its Relationship to the Church of the New Testament, with Particular Emphasis on the Kabbalah* (*Philosophie der Geschichte oder über die Tradition in dem alten Bunde und ihre Beziehung zur Kirche des neuen Bundes, mit vorzüglicher Rücksicht auf die Kabbalah*) in four volumes, published between 1827 and 1853. The book, which belongs to the "buried literature" of the nineteenth century, took a giant step toward prolonging the Goethean impulse, and was later forgotten with the advent of materialism and positivism. In his own time, Rudolf Steiner called attention to this important thinker and encouraged others to study him. But as far as I know, Molitor remained unknown, as did the few who did research on his work.

And yet, Molitor and his works were highly appreciated at the time in well-educated circles. The esoteric orientation of this thinking should have attracted some attention and could be expected to produce some interest in anthroposophical circles, so as to complete the change that has begun in Christian circles.

If I turn my attention to him, it is as an example of a capacity for spiritual respect and appreciation of Judaism. I don't necessarily want to create a following for his style, which is a mixture of theological and philosophical language, but I believe that the encounter with this author can fruitfully clarify our own ideas. Molitor is more than a curiosity, more than just one of the many eccentrics of which German history is full.

His entire life's work was the cultivation of deep mutual knowledge of Judaism and Christianity through the use of Hebrew sources, and it continues to open new perspectives on a future renewal of religion. Molitor thinks with devotion. He was a religious thinker in the best sense of the term, whose work awakens a faculty buried deep in ourselves, transcending the separation between faith and knowledge. Although his work will no doubt feel to some like an example of "pre-modernism," this form of thought bears seeds for the future. His learning was unique in that it took place through direct contact with the bearers of traditional Orthodox Judaism. Anyone who knows the importance for Judaism of the oral tradition of Torah will particularly appreciate this informant who was himself taught by oral transmission. His knowledge of the Torah, the Talmud, and the Kabbalah was enormous for a non-Jew. It is virtually impossible to know now who the kabbalists and Talmud scholars were with whom he studied for almost forty years . . . sketching out a conception of history that still moves us today by its warmth, its love for truth, and its strong faith. Molitor was unquestionably welcomed in the esoteric rabbinical milieu near his home in southern Germany. How this Catholic believer and practicing Freemason won the trust of Jewish orthodox scholars remains an open question, although it is tantalizing to wonder about the intentions of the kabbalists who initiated this Christian into a teaching that was in no way run of the mill in their own (Jewish) world. There are too few documents for us to have a clear picture of these relationships, or even to get a clear picture of this extraordinary man himself.

It would also be interesting to know the precise contributions of the rabbinic scholars to the elaboration of this monumental work for which Molitor, who lacked the means for such a meticulous work, was able to get financial support from Schelling and Baader. Despite his close relationship with Jewish orthodoxy, in which he found what was still a live spiritual tradition worth defending, Molitor was also—and simultaneously—open to the Reform current of Judaism that was then being born in Germany.

## PHILOSOPHY OF HISTORY AS JUDAIC PHILOSOPHY

Molitor's four volumes encompass many things: a complete philosophy of history, with solid contributions to philological research about Hebrew terminology; chronological sources; and a catalogue of sources. It is first and foremost a compendium of kabbalistic teachings, which had until then remained unavailable in that form in Germany.

His work was immediately praised by scholars of all origins, but some of his contributions on aspects of Jewish tradition were not fully appreciated until much later. Information on kabbalistic theory was often underestimated by Enlightenment philosophers, as well as by nineteenth-century Jewish scholars, who described it as a gnostic import alien to authentic Jewish esoteric traditions.

Molitor's work was openly considered a standard for specialists of the Kabbalah like Adolphe Franck,[4] who were working directly from the primary sources. Molitor's thoughts on Jewish tradition, both exoteric and esoteric, were not treated in the "cold," objective style of the scholar looking at myths and rituals from the outside. He openly defends as his own the cause of Judaism and the Kabbalah. He thinks with it, within it, and through it. For him, the entirety of Jewish history and religion was still alive. The Kabbalah, conceived as "the soul of souls" (the expression comes from the *Zohar*), was the center of one stream of sacred history whose origins are to be sought in the far reaches of humanity. This fund of wisdom was revealed to Adamic humanity, constantly renewed through historical epochs, and remains present in them. Tradition is the key to the meaning of history both Jewish and Christian, indeed to all history.

---

4. Adolphe Franck, *Die Kabbalah oder die Religionsphilosophie der Hebräer*, Leipzig, 1844. Reprint—Verlag, Leipzig O.J.

Molitor presents in two ways the teachings, concepts and myths he finds at the roots of Jewish tradition. He looks for the semantic origins of central concepts in the anthropology, cosmology, and hermeneutics of the Talmud and Kabbalah. He made available many primary sources that had hitherto only been available to Orthodox Jews (this is still mostly the case nowadays) and he cast light on their value as historical sources. Interestingly, his approach took him far beyond the familiar speculations of German Idealism.

His style is close to Schelling's and Baader's, and expresses in the abstract language of German idealism the esoteric quintessence and spirit of the mysteries. The latter of course is unthinkable without the contributions of authors like Jakob Boehme, Gottfried Arnold Oetinger, and Bengel, themselves quite close to the Kabbalah. Despite this fundamental kinship, which Habermas among others has pointed out,[5] most German Idealists remained prisoners of old conceptual schemes in relation to Judaism.[6]

## GERMAN IDEALISTS AND JEWS

Molitor's exceptional position is especially evident (compared with that of the German Idealists). For Kant, the Jews were "a nation of merchants ... the largest number of whom pledge allegiance to an old superstition tolerated by the states in which they live; they do not attempt to live like gentlemen but instead make up for their losses by duping the peoples under the protection of whom they live, or even by duping their own." Although the words have acquired a different load in the meantime, it still has a very unpleasant ring when Kant states "... the complete extinction of Judaism, the abandon-

---

5. J. Habermas, "Der deutsche Idealismus der Jüdischen Philosophen" in *Philosophisch-politische Profile*, 1971.
6. Franz von Baader was the only one among the German Idealists who never evidenced any trace of anti-Semitism.

ment of all its old precepts, would be the pure moral religion....["7]

Similarly, the following statement by Fichte was meant metaphorically, but one can understand Goldhagen's lumping him together with "exterminating anti-Semites" when we read his suggestion about "cutting off their head at night and replacing it with another head without a single Jewish idea in it."[8]

Even Hegel cannot escape scrutiny—despite his great merits elsewhere. In an early book, he displays total blindness toward the spiritual dimension of Judaism and the Jews:

> It is with this ragtag band of Jews that (Jesus') attempt to give them the consciousness of something divine failed: for the faith in something great cannot live in the dung. Just as the lion will not fit into a walnut, the infinite spirit has not room enough in a Jewish soul.[9]

For the later Hegel, Christianity was put in the saddle by the universal spirit, and Jews can at best "serve as its basket-carriers." For him, too, universal history has bypassed Judaism. Even the later Schelling, who supported and appreciated Molitor's work, has some strange formulas such as: "Impiety is the main characteristic of Mosaism."[10] Molitor's position is thus radically different from that of those great philosophers who continue to follow the unreflective compulsions of segregation, exclusion, and denigration. Unlike them, he takes seriously, without any reservation, the eternal mission of Judaism as it was announced by Paul (Romans, 11).

"It is conceivable that Yisrael is blind." (In his piety, Molitor transcribes all Hebrew names in their original sounding and

7. I. Kant, *Religion innerhalb der Grenzen der bloßen Vernunft*, as quoted in Rolf E. Schütt, *Von der jüdischen Philosophie zur deutschen Philosophie und zurück*, 1922, p. 9.
8. J. G. Fichte, *Beiträge zur Berichtigung der Urteile der französischen Revolution*, op. cit.
9. G. W. F. Hegel, *Theologische Jugendschriften*, in Schütt, op. cit.
10. E. W. J. Schelling, *Philosophie der Offenbarung*, op. cit., p. 10.

spelling, thus "Yisrael.")[11] Conceivably, the Jews fail to recognize that Jesus is the "Mashiach" they were expecting; nonetheless, Yisrael remains the people of a God that chose it as his own till the end of times. This frame of mind underlies this entire work and provides the guidelines of his philosophy of Christian and eschatological history.

In conclusion, and to stimulate further thought, I would like to quote some passages from this monumental work to call attention to Molitor's main ideas. It is important that the reader have access to the content and mood of the original, even if I can only reproduce extracts here. Molitor's phrases have a very characteristic style, imbued with deep faith, and a total love for truth. The purity of Molitor's thinking and of its expression are even more striking if one puts these passages in context. But his work is hard to find. The four volumes of the *Philosophy of History* are only accessible in a few copies of an 1853 edition. To the best of my knowledge, no new edition or even anthology is currently planned.[12]

## IDEAS AND EXTRACTS

For Molitor, the history, the nation, and the tradition of Israel are exemplars of the evolution of humanity as a whole as well as of the individual's spiritual evolution.

The history of oral tradition in the nation of Israel is the history of its (divine) guidance and spiritual evolution. The origin and the divine guidance of the Jewish nation constitute the main stream and central articulation of human history after the Fall:

Yisrael, as a reflection of human history in miniature, gives

---

11. "All these names should be pronounced in Hebrew" (F. J. Molitor, *Philosophie der Geschichte*, 1).
12. For other aspects of Molitor's work and importance, see: Christoph Schulz, *Franz Joseph Molitors Philosophie des Judentums*, in *Menora Jahrbuch für deutsch-jüdische Geschichte*, Munich, 1995.

us in the history of its election and later guidance a picture
of humanity's mystical life and inner evolution.

## FROM ADAM TO ABRAHAM: THE CENTRAL MYSTERY OF HUMANITY

From Adam to Noah, the course of primordial revelation is
at work throughout humanity and among the multitude of
nations. With the fall of Noah's kin, it became necessary to
extract the revelational nucleus out of the collectivity and provide for it esoterically by entrusting it to one family only—
Abraham's. The priestly house of Shem, going through Abraham and his descendants, streams into a continuum within
which original revelation could be transmitted in the future.

> In the mysteries of Shem's children ... the original doc-
> trine of monotheism was retained in all its purity. None-
> theless, it was also still a natural cult.... The family
> descended from Shem and Eber represents the great mys-
> tical human being; it is the most central organ and the
> most interiorized center of life ... Shem and Eber's lineage
> is, as it were, the lifeline of humanity....

Contrary to most Christians of his time, Molitor never
stopped extolling the merits of the Semites as against the Japhe-
ists, that is, the Indo-Germanic nations descended from Japhet.
The latter were active externally in the full breadth and length
of human doing; although still endowed with a remnant of the
original revelation, as a result of the iniquity of Noah's children
they were no longer able to carry the central mystery of humankind. Only Shem and his descendants can do that. When, in its
evolution after the flood, humanity entered adolescence
(according to a view of history that distinguishes infancy, adolescence, maturity, and old age), Noah had become the precursor of
individual consciousness, but the failings of his descendants who

abandoned the path of evolution as indicated by God made it necessary for humanity's spiritual guides to isolate the Semites, from whom Abraham was eventually descended. For Molitor, by virtue of being isolated, the Semites were chosen.

> Regarding future salvation and the regathering of the dispersed members of the great human being, who must be raised again in its new supranatural essence ... had it not been for humanity's repeated sinning and turning away from God, the church of God would not have needed to be reserved to Yisrael, but the entire human race would have formed one single body.
>
> But this isolation becomes necessary for historical salvation and it must be understood as an act destined for all humanity ... for if the children of Noah had not sinned, the seventy generations would have received the holy Earth as a communal holding and the whole Earth would have been transformed into Paradise.

## The Revelation at Sinai as the Work of the Holy Spirit

The revelation on Sinai is the descent of the Holy Spirit. It is the symmetrical image of the revelation of Pentecost that was experienced by the disciples after the death and resurrection of Christ.

> It is a restoration of the original law, whose purity was altered in the souls.... In the commandments at Sinai, and in the history of the people of God, the church of Christ is prefigured in its entirety and in its whole future development until the end of time.

## Late Judaism: Not an "externalization"

The later course of Israel's evolution (from Joshua and the Judges to David, through the Prophets, the Babylonian captivity and Ezra's and Nehemiahs' reforms) is the progressive revelation of the mysteries, each stage having its own integrity. The apparent intellectualization and the codifications of later epochs are merely external aspects of the necessary inner process toward the deepening of divine substance in the recesses of soul. They should not be interpreted as superficial or merely external processes.

> If we look at the time of Ezra from such a lofty perspective, even though the people of Yisrael may seem to have stepped backward, they had in fact progressed inwardly to a higher stage in their education…albeit marked by human weakness, the regulations bear the divine imprint. How else could humanity have understood the Mashiach?
>
> Religious education and the edification of the heart were always the core of Judaism, as well as of Christianity. This is what distinguished this religion from all other religions of antiquity. In pagan religions, there is a strict boundary between the exoteric and the esoteric realms.… But in Judaism, there was only a very discreet line between the two, making possible the gradual passage from one to the other.

It is on this basis that Molitor considers Judaism capable of evolving—Molitor who always bears in mind post-Christic Judaism, emphasizes this capacity for evolution.[13] He emphatically rejected ideas according to which Judaism was merely a legalistic religion, a conception that has reigned in the heart of Christianity until quite recently.

---

13. This ability to evolve is probably Molitor's major difference from Enlightenment philosophy: as described in Ralf Sonnenberg's article in these pages, no matter how benign their attitude toward Judaism may have been, they took for granted Jews' immutable nature. [Editor's note: MS]

### THE MASHIACH'S PASSION — POST-CHRISTIC JUDAISM

The destiny of the Jews as the paradigmatic people appears under a new light in the perspective of the cross of Golgotha and its nonacknowledgment. An important chapter of the philosophy of history deals with the Jews' refusal to see in Jesus the Mashiach. As a Christian, Molitor regrets that rejection. But he does not draw from it the usual conclusions: that Jews henceforth were excluded from the process of salvation in connection with the redemption of Jesus Christ. In accordance with the internal logic of Molitor's Christian and eschatological reflection, it is the complete opposite. This non-acknowledgment is part and parcel of the history of salvation, of the economy of salvation in its tragic impenetrability. From his point of view, Yisrael continues to live like a small humanity progressing toward its own purification, parallel to Christian evolution.

> The reason for this rejection of the foundation stone by God's people is buried in deep mystery. It is a fertile mystery, a chastening, not only for the Jews who crucified Christ, but for all of human nature, for all have had to fulfill the mystery. God veiled the Mashiach's prophecy, plunged it into enigmatic shadows to which one day the free human soul would gain access....
>
> The killing of the man-god is an abomination, as abominable as if it had been an individual's deed. The Jewish people is a mirror in which we should look at ourselves. All natural human beings continually reject and crucify Christ the Lord. Instead of piling the responsibility for this sin on the Jews and on the Jews alone, we should assume its burden with them. By projecting this sin again and again onto the backs of the Jewish people, we pretend to be the just, pretend that we would have done better. Such an attitude is an abomination in God's eyes.

## THE INNER MESSIAH

Molitor's meditations on the history of salvation culminate in a few words that illuminate a spiritual understanding of the Christ event that leaves behind any distinction between Jews and non-Jews.[14]

Natural human beings, whether Jewish or non-Jewish, want a natural, non-spiritual Mashiach.

The deeper spiritual significance of the Mashiach can only be recognized in impotence. Only by taking upon ourselves this impotence do we acquire the vision and the ability to recognize the spiritual Christ and give him a dwelling within us.

Shimon ben Shetach said: When seeking Truth, question thoughtfully. Choose your words carefully: A shrewd listener can detect your bias and through your words, learn to lie.

The "truths" we desire support what we already know. We become victims of our own opinions and rationalizations.

The Truth we need frees us from the known, makes us simple, and plants us firmly in Reality.

1:9

(From the *Pirke Avot*)

---

14. Rudolf Steiner takes an identical stand in *Bausteine zu einer Erkenntnis des Mysterium von Golgotha*, GA 175, April 24, 1917, Dornach, 1982, p. 336 ff.

# 14

# Against a Return to Normality

ACCUSATIONS OF ANTI-SEMITISM AS AN
OCCASION FOR SELF-EXAMINATION

## by Dirk Lorenz

*from* Info 3, *June 2000*

*translated and edited by Mado Spiegler*

I FEEL SOMEWHAT IRRITATED by the constant repetition of basically the same defenses, coming from people intent on "protecting" Rudolf Steiner's work and even his person....

There is something desperate about this "defense" of Rudolf Steiner. Phrases like "taken out of context," or "turbulences in the stenogram" (*Info3*/2000) make me feel that I am reading a politician's denial. The question is not whether the arguments advanced (in defense of Rudolf Steiner) are in themselves true or false. Their falseness comes rather from their desperate, pouting, self-righteous quality. "It just can't be true!" (... As long as) the very act of looking for answers is fearfully avoided... as long as we think it just a matter of deciding the bare truth of the accusations, and be done with them, no matter how much we dig in (Steiner's) works, we won't get any further. The obsessive preoccupation with the issue hides a fearful desire to avoid any questioning at all. And where there is fear, as depth psychology tells us, there is a real issue.

In fact, what would really make the discussion interesting would be to ask the following question: Could it conceivably be that, seen from today's perspective, Steiner's thought *did* contain anti-Semitic, racist elements? The question is an important one, for we stand at a juncture where the answer will determine the reception of Steiner's work today and in the future,

Let me take as an example the cult of the personality that has developed around Steiner. How is my stance toward Steiner's work affected by my celebrating his birthday, the anniversary of his death, having his picture on my wall... to what extent do these things hinder me or those who are under my care? Or again: how does a person receive Steiner's work if it comes accompanied by the cult of Steiner's personality, let alone if this cult is allowed to influence pedagogical situations?

Critics of anthroposophy will rightly continue to probe the wound if, whenever the accusation of racism or religious intolerance comes up, the cry goes up "Not true! Not true!" meaning "it can't be true," and under our breath, "we cannot allow it to be true." What point is there in commissioning research about a subject, if I have decided ahead of time what the results must be!

In the article about Rudolf Steiner and Judaism in *Info3*, April 2000, we find a quote that was cited by the Dutch commission. Steiner's biographer Lindenberg was called to the rescue on that one. The Steiner quote (from an 1888 book review) says the following: "Judaism as such has outlived itself, it has no justification in the modern life of nations, and its having survived at all is a mistake of world history, which will inevitably have consequences."

The quote is especially painful now, when the "inevitable consequences" are associated with something that at the time of the pronouncement lay still in the future. We link it with the Holocaust, and rightly so.

It would be fruitful to go to the bottom of that link, and it could lead us to some truths, the further exploration of which would be quite rewarding. But the reflexive recourse to interpretations that merely befog the issue ("taken out of context") appeals to the same frame of mind that leads others to use these quotes to declare Steiner a precursor of the Holocaust.

Within this frame of mind the search for truth is forever stopped by the desire for "easy" answers.

It is too easy to call the phrase a "derailing," as Lindenberg does, or to say as the Dutch study does that "it is put a little too sharply." Both descriptions strike me as frightfully minimizing. I personally would rather protect Steiner from such distorted, posthumous good intentions.

"Derailing"? How? When someone goes off the track, something slips out that the person thinks but didn't intend to say. Or else something is said that had actually not been intended. Surely, whether it is one or the other makes a difference.

"Formulated too sharply"? Anyone who goes for that version should make an exercise: how would this statement sound if expressed more softly!

If it weren't for the momentous consequences of this desperate refusal to face facts, we might find it moving or a little tragi-comic. But anthroposophy is not a sect that feeds on its own juice: it is made of human beings who are active, human beings who claim to act out of spiritual impulses. Furthermore, to the extent that we work in the pedagogical or curative field, our actions have very large consequences. This is why we cannot afford a faintheartedness that keeps us stuck in a realm of foggy-thinking enthusiasm. We will pay the price for it, but even more importantly, the human beings entrusted to us in anthroposophical schools, anthroposophical curative and therapeutic institutions, will pay for it, too, and we have a duty to protect them from all the things whose existence we wrongheadedly insist cannot possibly exist among us, for instance, racism.

One subtext of the defensive reactions to accusations of racism is the defensive affirmation that "just because we insist on the Jews 'difference' from the rest of us—for instance, they really don't believe in Christ—doesn't mean that we would send anyone to the gas chambers." Having reassured ourselves in this way, we can let things "return to normal," now that the Holocaust is over.

There can't be any such a thing as "normality," and we are not just talking about the Holocaust. What we must understand is that "normality," "things as normal," can no longer exist, and not just in relation to the Jews. For "normality" is the normality of the exclusion of other human beings, the normality of religious, ethnic, and cultural intolerance.

To the extent that a person lives his or her life out of a religious faith, he or she must fully experience the tension between religious faith and tolerance—and tolerance is the demand of our time. Tolerance consists in more than refraining from murdering each other: it reaches much further. Tolerance itself must become unnecessary, for tolerance is by definition granted by one person to another; it is a dubious and at best temporary stage on the way to a truly fraternal life. Rudolf Steiner was quite clear on the subject. That is why he predicted the death of great religious organizations. But we misunderstand him when we understand this death of organizations as merely the disappearance of organizational structures. According to Steiner, the very "matter" that holds organizations together will disappear, that is, the idea of belief as organized, and an organizing social force, an intransigent ('terrorist') conception of truth (*Wahrheitsterror*). What this means is that anthroposophy and the Christian Community are in no way immune to this fate. Many of us would like to believe that things are more or less safe for us, since—unlike the established church—anthroposophy is only "loosely structured" (whatever the euphemism may mean). But this reassurance may actually cover up and defend all the more fiercely a clinging dependence on faith (*Bekenntnishaftigkeit*) enforced by suprapersonal social controls.

# Biographies

SCHMUEL HUGO BERGMAN (1883-1975) met Rudolf Steiner in Prague in 1905. He was a member of the Humanist Zionist *Bar Kochba*; a student and collaborator of Martin Bube; founder and longtime director of the Hebrew National Library; first Rector of the University of Jerusalem; and professor of philosophy. His dialogical philosophy spans Christian Theology, Rudolf Steiner, Martin Buber, Franz Rosenzweig, and Aurobindo. He is the author of *Dialogical Philosophy from Kierkegaard to Buber*, SUNY Press,1991.

HANS-JÜRGEN BRACKER is the editor of the journal *Novalis*, published in Schaffhausen, Switzerland.

JÁNOS DARVAS is a frequent contributor to *Die Drei* and *Info3* on the cultural history of Central Europe, the preliminaries and history of the Holocaust and the relation between eso teric traditions.

SHIMON LEVY teaches theater in Israel and England. He is the creator of a highly original approach to the Bible as dramaturgy and a noted interpreter of Samuel Beckett's plays. He is the author of *The Bible as Theatre* and *Samuel Beckett's Self-Referential Drama: the Sensitive Chaos*.

RUDI LISSAU is a regular contributor to the *Golden Blade*, published in England. He is author of *Rudolf Steiner—An Introduction; Rudolf Steiner's Social Intentions;* and coauthor of *The Challenge of the Will.*

GÜNTHER RÖSCHERT was head of cultural services for foreign immigrants in the city of Munich. He is a contributor to *Die Drei* and *Anthroposophische Kritik.* and author of the German book *Fur die Sache Gottes—Der Islam in anthroposophischer Sicht.*

JOHANNES SCHNEIDER is a longtime Waldorf school teacher. He also teaches psychology and counseling for teachers and geriatric caretakers. He is the author of *Träume besser verstehen* and *Vom Sinn und Wert der Laebenskrisen.*

DAVID SCHWEITZER is a lawyer and legal writer in Basel, Switzerland. He is President of the Zionist Association in Basel and a member of the Friedrich Nietzsche Branch of the Anthroposophical Society.

RALF SONNENBERG specializes in the history of German nineteenth- and twentieth-century Religion. His focus has been the representation and critique of race, nation, and ethnicity, and the development of the international eugenic movement and anti-Semitism, particularly in the context of Rudolf Steiner's work on history as individuation process. He is a regular contributor to *Die Drei, Anthroposophische Kritik,* and *Info3.*

ROLF UMBACH writes on Kabbala and Christianity. He is the author of *Vom Flug der Fischen. Die Bibel kabbalistisch gelesen.*

GERHARD WEHR trained to be a priest. Active many years as adult educator and social worker, he now teaches social pedagogy. He is the author of many books on religious and spiritual history, including biographies of C.G.Jung, Meister Eckhart, Martin Buber, Jakob Boehme and Rudolf Steiner. His book on C.G. Jung and Rudolf Steiner was translated as *Jung and Steiner: The Birth of a New Psychology,* Anthroposophic Press, 2002.

# Bibliography

This bibliography is an attempt to let Judaism explain itself. It does not include the multitude of books written by those outside Judaism that interpret it from their perspective.

The bibliography is divided into two sections. The first section will list some of Judaism's foundational works. Because there is so little knowledge of these works in the Christian and secular worlds, a few statements about them will be in order—all but one or two will be by Jewish scholars.

The second section will list a few contemporary works dealing with the different aspects of Judaism. Because of the vast number of these books in the library, I am reduced to mainly listing my favorites, some of the ones that have proved most important in my study of Judaism.

According to the ancient rabbis, the world rests on three pillars — study, worship, and good deeds. But the greatest of these is study, because from study the others can be deduced.

And what does one study? One studies *Torah*. Here a great misunderstanding can occur. Torah, from the King James Version of the Bible on, has usually been translated as *Law*, though a more accurate translation would be *instruction*. But even here one is likely to understand it too narrowly. Torah has many levels of meaning. It can refer to the first five books of the Bible. It can refer in an expanded sense to the Hebrew Bible as a whole. But it can also refer to more than one text or book: it can refer to "the entire revelation and the entire activity of Jewish study throughout the generations ... (in fact) it can be said that all Jewish study is Torah and all Torah has the validity of revelation. Its authority rests with God, but its agents are human beings. Throughout time Jews have always seen their primary occupation as being part of this devotion to study, this ongoing revelation." (Barry Holtz)

We can picture Torah as an inverted pyramid with the Bible at its base, expanded outwardly through the Mishnah, the Talmuds, the commentaries, the legal codes, the mystical tradition, the philosophical books, and the Midrashic literature. (Holtz) We are also reminded that there is a cosmological level in interpreting the concept of Torah. According to a Midrash, God looked into Torah to create the world. (Rabbi Arthur Green) In other words, God needed Torah as a blueprint in order to create the world. One can see here how the close connection between Torah and "Wisdom" (Chokmah-Sophia) developed.

## Foundational Works

### INTRODUCTIONS TO FOUNDATIONAL JEWISH WORKS

1. Akenson, Donald Harman. *Surpassing Wonder: The Invention of the Bible and the Talmuds.* Covers the Hebrew scriptures, the *Mishnah*, the Tosefta, Sifra, and the Jerusalem and Babylonian Talmuds. A most fascinating work.

2. Holtz, Barry W. (ed.). *Back to the Sources: Reading the Classic Jewish Texts.* The first complete modern guide to the great books of the Jewish tradition: what they are and how to read then, written by today's leading scholars.

3. Neusner, Jacob. *Introduction to Rabbinic Literature.* Detailed study of the great rabbinic works of the first seven centuries of the Common Era. For the serious student.

4. Levenson, Jon. *Sinai and Zioni: An Entrance into the Jewish Bible.*

5. —— *The Hebrew Bible, The Old Testament, and Historical Criticism.*

## THE BASIC TEXT: THE JEWISH BIBLE

1. *Tanakh: The Holy Scriptures.* The new JPS (Jewish Publication Society) translation according to the traditional Hebrew text (1985). The word "Tanakh" is an acronym for the three divisions of the Jewish Bible: *Torah*—the first five books of the Bible; *Nevi'im*—the prophets (this includes books that Christians are likely to see as "historical"—such as Joshua and 1 & 2 Samuel); and *Kethuvim*—the writings. This section starts with Psalms and ends with 1& 2 Chronicles, and includes all the books not in the *Torah* and *Nevi'im*. Though the *Tanakh* and the Christian "Old Testament" contain the same books, they are arranged differently And, embedded in the different arrangements is the key not only to the different interpretations of the Hebrew Bible within the two communities, but to the different directions that Rabbinic Judaism and Christianity took as two branches rooted in the same trunk. (Donald Akenson; Arthur Green; Alan Segal)

2. *Die Schrift: Die hebraische Bibel.* Verdeutscht von Martin Buber gemeinsam mit Franz Rosenzweig. Vier Bände. (This is the famous translation by Martin Buber and Franz Rosenzweig, where they attempt to translate the Bible into German in such a way that the original Hebrew words, with their multileveled meanings as well as Hebrew syntax becomes as transparent as possible.)

3. *The Schocken Bible: volume 1. The Five Books of Moses.* (A new translation with introductions, commentary, and notes by Everett Fox.) Fox does in English for the first five books of the Hebrew Bible what Buber and Rosenzweig did in German for the whole of it. One can almost feel the rumble and roar of the ancient Hebrew behind the English. It is a totally different experience than one has in reading any other translation.

## THE MISHNAH

The *Mishnah* is the first standardized compilation of Rabbinic teachings (approximately 220 C.E.). It is mostly devoted to halachah material. But even so, it is a most strange and difficult document. To quote Donald Akenson, "the heart of Rabbinic Judaism is a text that is one of the most mysterious one can encounter, for it hides its secrets in plain sight, the most cunning form of camouflage." This is the *Mishnah*, a term that comes from the verb *shanah*, meaning to repeat, to learn, to teach, to study and to heed oral instruction." He then goes on to describe it as "forbidding, enticing, obvious, impenetrable, seductive, vexing, and all at once." And it cannot be anything other, seeing that it is an attempt to reinvent the Tanakh by rebuilding the destroyed Temple—but this time in the minds and hearts of the Jewish people.

1. *The Mishnah*. A new translation by Jacob Neusner.
2. Neusner, Jacob. *The Mishnah: An Introduction*.

## THE TALMUD

If one had to name a single document that distinguishes Judaism from all other faiths, it would be the Babylonian Talmud. "No book in the history of Judaism, not even the Bible, has had the formative influence of the Talmud. Everything in the history of Judaism that predates the Talmud seems incomplete and unfinished, while everything that comes after the Talmud seems a mere supplement to it." (Ben Zion Bokser) The word "Talmud," from the root "lamed," refers to the whole of the Mishnah section by section, followed by its commentary, the "Gammer." Given that there are two distinct "Gemarot" (pl.), there are also two different Talmuds: the Palestinian (also called the Jerusalem Talmud, or the *Yerushalmi*) and that of Babylonia (usually referred to as the *Bavli*). The Babylonian commentary is clearer and much more complete than that of the Jerusalem, and is by far the best

known. Therefore, when people speak of "the Talmud," they are almost always referring to the Babylonian Talmud. Like the biblical text, the text of the Talmud is made up of two categories of texts that are completely interwoven. The first category is that of *Halachah*, the part dealing with practical action (usually defined as the "legal" section) and the second that of *Aggadah*.

Unfortunately, the library does not have an edition of the multivolume Talmud (now available in several excellent English translations). We do have a couple of volumes of excerpts:

1. Bokser, Ben Zion (ed.). *The Talmud. Selected Writings.* (CWS)
2. Cohen, Abraham. *Everyman's Talmud: The Major Teachings of the Rabbinic Sages.*

The problem with these is that the pages are not set up in the unique style of the original Talmud. In the original, the way the pages are laid out gives one a glimpse of the great difference between the Rabbinic Jewish way of thinking and the thinking of the Greek philosophers, and thus modern Western thought.

Introductions to Talmudic Study:

1. Abrams, Judith Z. *The Talmud for Beginners, vol. 1. Prayer.*
2. Kraemer, David. *The Mind of the Talmud.*
3. Rosen, Jonathan. *The Talmud and the Internet. A Journey between Two Worlds.* (A glorious little book—fun and profound at the same time.)

## HALAKHAH

The Hebrew root of the word means "to walk." Thus it can be said that *Halakhah* refers to 'walking in God's truth' the normative path trodden by those who wish to follow God's will, the life prescribed by Torah as fulfilled in the context of real, ongoing, and evolving human community. (Arthur Green)

Three major Halakhic works are:

1. Moses Maimonides, *The Codes* (12th century).
2. Jacob ben Asher, *Arba'ah Turim* (*Four Columns*), 18th century.
3. Joseph Caro, *Shulchan Aruch* (*Set Table*), 16th century.

These codifications may make *Halakhah* seem fixed and rigid, but one must remember that they came about through a living process. Many generations of sages worked on these codes, some taking great risks in their decisions on how to apply Torah to totally new situations. For an extraordinary modern explication of *Halakhah* I recommend *Halakhic Man*, by Rabbi Joseph B. Soloveitchik.

### AGGADAH

*Aggadah* is difficult to define. The simplest way to do it would be to say that the Aggadah is everything that is *not Halakhah.* "It covers not only homilies, the preaching and edifying exegesis of the Bible, things that speak to the heart in order to move, to the mind in order to persuade; but we can also find real or legendary history as well as notions about the most varied sciences. We can also find discussions on dream symbols and their interrelation, different ideas about the end of time, the Messianic era, the resurrection of the dead, and so on." (Marc-Alain Ouaknin, *The Burnt Book: Reading the Talmud.*)

1. *The Book of Legends* (Sefer Ha-Aggadah): *Legends from the Talmud and Midrash* (ed. Hayim Nahman Bialik and Yehoshua Hana Ravitzky).
2. Ginzberg, Louis. *The Legends of the Jews* (7 vols.)

### MIDRASH

If, when it comes to texts, the Talmud is what distinguishes Jewish spirituality from all others, then concerning the inter-

pretation of texts, *Midrash* is the method of interpretation—the hermeneutic—that distinguishes Jewish spirituality. "Midrash (from the Hebrew root "to seek out," "to go in pursuit of"), which contains both legendary and legal material, is both a process and a product (the results of Midrashic interpretation are also referred to as Midrash). It reflects the process of searching the text of Scripture in order to better understand it and apply it to life." (Reuven Hammer) One must not think of Midrash as just a method of exegesis but also as a form of life; its concern is not just with meaning—really, the *creation* of meaning—but also with action in the world. Ithamar Gruen-wald states it precisely: "Midrash is a vital instrument in creat-ing patterns of perception, conceptualization, and realization in which scriptural terms of reference are applied for existential purposes." This mental attitude can be extended to all aspects of life that call for interpretation.

Midrash as a procedure is found in the Mishnah and the Talmud, and as a product in a series of ancient commentaries on the Bible. Of these midrashic commentaries, the library has only one anthology:

*The Classic Midrash: Tannaitic Commentaries on the Bible.* Translation, introduction, and commentaries by Reuven Hammer, with a preface by Judah Goldin. "Tannaitic" refers to the "Tannaim," the name given to a group of early rabbis, starting with the disciples of Hillel and Shammai, and continuing for a couple of hundred years (until 220 CE).

Introductions to Midrash:

1. One of the best short introductions is by Gerald Bruns: *Midrash and Allegory: The Beginnings of Scriptural Interpretation,* found in *The Literary Guide to the Bible,* ed. Robert Alter and Frank Kermode.

2. The best short introductory volume on interpreting the Hebrew Scriptures, with an emphasis on Midrash, is: *The*

*Way into Torah,* by Norman J. Cohen. This is a volume in an extraordinary series of books designed to introduce people to different aspects of Judaism, published by Jewish Lights Press (*The Way Into...* series).

Other introductory works:

1. Boyarin, Daniel. *Intertextuality and the Reading of Midrash.*
2. Fishbane, Michael, ed. *The Midrashic Imagination: Jewish Exegesis, Thought, and History.*
3. Halivni, David Weiss. *Peshat and Derash: Plain and Applied Meaning in Rabbinic Exegesis.*
4. Kugel, James L. and Rowanai Greer. *Early Biblical Interpretation.*
5. Neusner, Jacob. *The Midrash: An Introduction.*
6. Ouaknin, Marc-Alain. *The Burnt Book: Reading the Talmud.* A post-modern exploration of Midrash. One of the most exciting books ever, but not for the faint of heart.

## MYSTICISM

Because of the role Gnosticism plays in it, there is not the large gap between mysticism and esotericism in Jewish thought that there is in Christianity. Anthroposophists should keep this in mind.

Basic Texts:

1. The *Zohar*—attributed to Moses de Leon of Granada, Spain (thirteenth century). The fundamental book of Jewish Kabbalism. Written in the form of a commentary on the Pentateuch. One needs the guidance of an adept in order to gain an understanding of it. The library has both the five-volume translation by Harry Sperling and Maurice Simon, and the acclaimed abridgement by Daniel Matt in the *Classics of Western Spirituality* series.

2. The *Sepher ha Bahir*—("Book of Brilliance"). (Edited in the twelfth century mostly out of far older materials. The first appearance of the "tree of life"—the ten sefirot.)

3. The *Sepher Yetzirah: The Book of Creation*. Edited and with commentary by Aryeh Kaplan. The earliest of Kabbalistic texts; references to this work, according to some, appeared already in the first century C.E. Even more obscure than the Zohar and the Bahir.

4. Vitalé, Chaim. *The Tree of Life.* Vitalé was the preeminent disciple of Isaac Luria (sixteenth century), one of the greatest mystics and esotericists the world has produced. Since Isaac Luria wrote almost nothing, this book is as close to his thought as one can get. When asked why he didn't write anything, he is reported to have said, "It is impossible, because all things are connected with one another. I can hardly open my mouth to speak without feeling as though the sea burst its dams and overflowed."

5. *Safed Spirituality: Rules of Mystical Piety, and the Beginning of Wisdom.* Edited by Lawrence Fine—Classics of Western Spirituality. It was in Safed, by the Sea of Galilee, that the greatest of the Kabbalists of the sixteenth century gathered around Isaac Luria—some of them having been driven out of Spain. This is a small selection of their work.

6. *The Early Kabbalah.* A selection of works from the twelfth century, edited and introduced by Joseph Dan. (Classics of Western Spirituality) Dan's introduction is most illuminating in its description of the connection of Gnosticism to Kabbalah.)

7. Schneur Zalman of Liadi—the *Tanya* (3 vols.) The major work of Habad Hasidism. An eighteenth-century reworking of Kabbalah with amazing mystical depth. Unfortunately, little known and read today outside Lubavitch circles. The best introduction to the *Tanya* and Habad Hasidism is Rachel Elior's *The Paradoxical Ascent to God.*

8. Two books on Messianic mysticism are:

   Cardozo, Abraham Miguel, *Selected Writings* (CWS).

   Scholem, Gershom, *Sabatai Sevi: The Mystical Messiah*. A monumental work.

## Some Important Commentaries on Kabbalah

1. Scholem, Gershom. *Major Trends in Jewish Mysticism*. The most basic and important of all works on Jewish mysticism. This work revolutionized all thought on Judaism.

2. Scholem, Gershom. *On the Kabbalah and Its Symbolism*.

3. Dan, Joseph. *Jewish Mysticism* (4 vols). One of Scholem's best disciples has put together in four large volumes essays on all aspects of Jewish mysticism that he has written over the years.

4. Green, Arthur (ed.). *Jewish Spirituality*, (2 vols).

5. Matt, Daniel. *The Essential Kabbalah*. A beautiful small volume of short abstracts on essential aspects of Kabbalah from basic texts.

6. Idel, Moshe. *Kabbalah—New Perspectives*. A different way of thinking about Kabbalah than Scholem's.

7. Müller, Ernst. *History of Jewish Mysticism*. A pre-Scholem history of Jewish mysticism by a prominent anthroposophist and close friend of Rudolf Steiner. Müller remained a practicing Jew while being an anthroposophist.

# Selected Books by Modern Jewish Writers on Various Aspects of Judaism

## Jewish Festivals, Spiritual Practices, and Meditation

*Judaism is not about creed, it is about calendar.*
—Harvey Cox

*Judaism is a religion of time, aiming at the sanctification of time.*
—Abraham J. Heschel

### Festivals

1. Benyosef, Simcha H. *Living the Kabbalah: A Guide to the Sabbath and the Festivals in the Teachings of Rabbi Rafael Moshe Luria.*

2. Cox, Harvey. *Common Prayers: Faith, Family, and a Christian's Journey through the Jewish Year.* A most extraordinary book. Here I let a Christian theologian speak for Judaism. How he does it from so deeply into Judaism is a mystery. Clearly, being married to a Jewish woman and raising a Jewish son have helped.

3. Greenberg, Irving. *The Jewish Way: Living the Holidays.* The best book on festivals, and one of the best introductions to Judaism.

4. Heschel, Abraham Joshua. *The Sabbath: Its meaning for Modern Man.*

5. Klagsbrun, Francine. *Jewish Days: a Book of Jewish Life and Culture around the Year.*

6. Schweid, Eliezer. *The Jewish Experience of Time: Philosophical Dimensions of the Jewish Holy Days.*

7. Ziff, Joel. *Mirrors in Time: A Psycho-Spiritual Journey through the Jewish Year.*

### Meditation

Recently, there has been an enormous output of books on Jewish meditation. I can only mention a few here:

1. Buxbaum, Yitzhak. *Jewish Spiritual Practices.*

2. Cooper, David. *God Is a Verb: Kabbalah and the Practice of Mystical Judaism.*

   ——*Renewing Your Soul: A Guided Retreat for the Sabbath and Other Days of Rest.*

3. Greenbaum, Avraham. *Under the Table and How to Get Up: Jewish Pathways of Spiritual Growth.* This is a book that will encourage *anyone* to try some of the great Jewish ways to fulfillment in life.

4. Kaplan, Aryeh. *Jewish Meditation.*

   ——*Meditation and Kabbalah.*

5. Shapiro, Rami. *Minyan: Ten Principles for Living a Life of Integrity.* Anything Rami Shapiro writes not only *can* be, but *should* be read by *everyone.* He has a way of writing out of Judaism for people of all traditions.

### CONTEMPORARY JEWISH PHILOSOPHICAL THOUGHT

Before going on to modern thinkers, I must mention the greatest of all Jewish philosophers and the prism through which all later Jewish philosophy has had to go—Maimonides, whose magnus opus is *Guide of the Perplexed.* In this work he does for Judaism what St. Thomas Aquinas did for Christianity, namely, incorporate Greek philosophy (via Aristotle) into his religious tradition.

There are so many great contemporary Jewish philosophical thinkers. All I can do is mention a few of my favorites, starting with the great postmodern French Jewish philosopher, Emmanuel Levinas.

### EMMANUEL LEVINAS :

1. *Nine Talmudic Readings.*
2. *Beyond the Verse: Talmudic Readings and Lectures.*

3. *Difficult Freedom: Essays on Judaism.*
4. *In the Time of Nations.*
5. *Of God Who Comes to Mind.*
6. *God, Death and Time.*

SUSAN HANDELMAN :

1. *Slayers of Moses: The Emergence of Rabbinic Interpretation in Modern Literary Theory.* Essential reading for all who are interested in modern literary criticism, and the philosophy of language in general.
2. *Fragments of Redemption: Jewish Thought and Literary Theory in Benjamin, Scholem and Levinas.*

ABRAHAM JOSHUA HESCHEL :

1. *God in Search of Man: A Philosophy of Judaism.*
2. *A Passion for Truth.*
3. *Between God and Man: An Interpretation of Judaism.*
4. *Moral Grandeur and Spiritual Audacity* (essays).

WALTER BENJAMIN :

1. *Illuminations: Essays and Reflection.*
2. *Reflections: Essays, Aphorisms, Autobiographical Writings.*

DAVID HARTMAN :

1. *Maimonides: Torah and Philosophic Quest.*
2. *A Living Covenant: The Innovative Spirit in Traditional Judaism.*
3. *A Heart of Many Rooms: Celebrating the Many Voices within Judaism.*

FRANZ ROSENZWEIG :

1. *Understanding the Sick and the Healthy: A View of World, Man and God.*
2. *The Star of Redemption.*

MARTIN BUBER :
1. *I and Thou.*
2. *The Prophetic Faith.*
3. *Between Man and Man.*
4. *Eclipse of God.*
5. *Hasidism and Modern Man.*

ARTHUR GREEN :
*Seek My Face, Speak My Name: A Contemporary Jewish Theology.* A wonderful starting point to enter quickly into contemporary liberal Jewish thought.

JON LEVENSON :
*Creation and the Persistence of Evil.* This is a major work on the question of evil as found in the Hebrew Bible.

DAVID BLUMENTHAL :
*Facing the Abusing God: A Theology of Protest.* A most disturbing book by a great rabbi who is also a philosopher and psychoanalyst.

### JUDAISM AND REINCARNATION

Two excellent overviews of life after death in Judaism:

1. Gilman, Neil. *The Death of Death: Resurrection and Immortality in Jewish Thought.*
2. Raphael, Simcha Paull. *Jewish Views of the Afterlife.*

Books dealing specifically with the concept of reincarnation:

1. Gershom, Yonassan. *Cases of Reincarnation from the Holocaust.*
   ——*From Ashes to Healing: Mystical Encounters with the Holocaust.*
   ——*Jewish Tales of Reincarnation*
2. Pinson, Dov Ber. *Reincarnation and Judaism: The Journey of the Soul.*

## ISRAEL AND ZIONISM

1. Armstrong, Karen. *Jerusalem: One City, Three Faiths.*
2. Idinopulos, Thomas A. *Weathered by Miracles: A History of Palestine from Bonaparte and Muhammed Ali to Ben-Gurion and the Mufti.*
3. Shlaim, Avi. *The Iron Wall: Israel and the Arab World.*
4. Sternhell, Zeev. *The Founding Myths of Israel.*

Finally, I must mention a most wonderful way into Jewish thought: through the great Hebrew words.

Green, Arthur. *These Are the Words: A Vocabulary of Jewish Spiritual Life.*

# THE MARK

One day the king summoned his counselor and told him of his anguish: "I have read in the stars that all those who will eat of the next harvest will be struck with madness. What shall we do, my friend?"

"Nothing could be more simple, Sire," replied the counselor, "we shall not touch it. Last year's harvest is not yet exhausted. You have but to requisition it; it will be ample for you. And me."

"And the others?" scolded the king. "All the subjects of my kingdom? The faithful servants of the crown? The men, the women, the madmen and the beggars, are you forgetting them? Are you forgetting the children, the children too?"

"I am forgetting nobody, Sire. But as your adviser, I must be realistic and take all possibilities into account. We don't have enough reserves, not enough to protect and satisfy everyone. There will be just enough for you. And me."

Thereupon the king's brow darkened, and he said: "Your solution does not please me. Is there no Other? Never mind. But I refuse to separate myself from my people and I don't care to remain lucid in the midst of a people gone mad. Therefore we shall all enter madness together. You and I like the others, with the others. When the world is gripped by delirium, it is senseless to watch from the outside: the mad will think that we are mad too. And yet, I should like to safeguard some reflection of our present glory and of our anguish too; I should like to keep alive the memory of this determination, this decision. I should like that when the time comes, you and I shall remain aware of our predicament."

"Whatever for, Sire?"

"It will help us, you'll see. And thus we shall be able to help our friends. Who knows, perhaps thanks to us, men will find the strength to resist later, even if it is too late." And putting his arm around his friend's shoulders, the king went on: "You and I shall therefore mark each other's foreheads with the seal of madness. And every time we shall look at one another, we shall know, you and I, that we are mad."

(Rebbe Nachman of Breslov)